THE G MAJOR VIOLIN SONATA
(*Bach's autograph*)

THE MUSIC OF
B A C H

AN
INTRODUCTION

By
CHARLES SANFORD TERRY

DOVER PUBLICATIONS, INC.
NEW YORK

Published in Canada by General Publishing Company, Ltd., 30 Lesmill Road, Don Mills, Toronto, Ontario.

Published in the United Kingdom by Constable and Company, Ltd., 10 Orange Street, London, WC 2.

This Dover edition, first published in 1963, is an unabridged and unaltered republication of the work first published by the Oxford University Press in 1933. This edition is published by special arrangement with the Oxford University Press.

Standard Book Number: 486-21075-8
Library of Congress Catalog Card Number: 63-19516

Manufactured in the United States of America
Dover Publications, Inc.
180 Varick Street
New York, N.Y. 10014

'*She played Bach. I do not know the names of the pieces, but I recognized the stiff ceremonial of the frenchified little German courts and the sober, thrifty comfort of the burghers, and the dancing on the village green, the green trees that looked like Christmas trees, and the sunlight on the wide German country, and a tender cosiness; and in my nostrils there was a warm scent of the soil and I was conscious of a sturdy strength that seemed to have its roots deep in mother earth, and of an elemental power that was timeless and had no home in space.*'

From 'The Alien Corn'
by W. SOMERSET MAUGHAM

To

ALBERT SCHWEITZER
THIS INADEQUATE EXPRESSION
OF PROFOUND REGARD

PREFATORY NOTE

A CENTURY and a quarter have passed since Samuel Wesley, Bach's ecstatic propagandist, wrote to Benjamin Jacob: 'I knew that you had only to know Bach to love and adore him, and I sincerely assure you that, in meeting so true an Enthusiast in so good a Cause (and depend on it that nothing very good or very great is done without enthusiasm), I experience a warmth of Heart which only enthusiasts know or can value.'

The enthusiasm and the demand in 1809 were for Bach's organ music—'The Organ is King, be the Blockheads never so unquiet' Samuel boasted jubilantly. Other aspects of him were shrouded by the mists of ignorance. To-day enthusiasm is general, the public appetite omnivorous. Bach, formerly frowned upon by the generality as academic, 'high-brow', 'a cold mathematical precisian', is now the idol of a widening public, which finds in his music the very qualities in which it was once supposed deficient.

These pages fill the gap deliberately left open in my *Bach: a Biography*. They offer a plain, non-technical guide to one of the largest expanses of musical thought planned by a human brain. I use the word 'guide' advisedly. For my purpose is indicative rather than expositive, to relate Bach's music to the circumstances of his life, unfold its extent, offer guidance for a more intensive study of it, and incidentally engender the 'warmth of Heart' of true enthusiasm.

I am much indebted to Herr Manfred Gorke for permission to reproduce the facsimile of Bach's autograph of the G major Violin Sonata, one of the principal treasures of his remarkable collection of Bachiana.

C. S. T.

WESTERTON OF PITFODELS,
Summer, 1932.

CONTENTS

I. THE CAREER AND THE MUSIC

IN a general way, the music of every composer in any age is the mirror of his circumstances, and more or less faithfully reflects them. Certainly this is so with Bach and his period. For the art of musical invention was not yet admitted to be the province of inspired minds, but was deemed the normal accomplishment of official musicians in executive posts. The Capellmeister at the princely court, the Cantor in his parochial church, were equally charged to furnish the organization they controlled with music of their own contriving. By no other means, indeed, could its needs be satisfied. Little instrumental music was in print and circulation, and of church music such as Bach wrote there was none. Nor were manuscript scores readily exchangeable. Bach was strongly disinclined to lend his own, and his prejudice was shared by others with less cause to deem them valuable, but equal reason to preserve them for their own occasions. Recognition outside their immediate circle consequently was the lot of few. The concert-room only afforded a platform for public music late in the eighteenth century, and at Leipzig Bach held himself aloof from it. Only rarely was he induced to provide music not required by the conditions of his office: the Brandenburg Concertos, the *Musical Offering* (*Musicalisches Opfer*) dedicated to Frederick the Great, and, perhaps, the funeral music for Prince Leopold of Anhalt-Cöthen, are the rare exceptions to an otherwise invariable rule of abstinence. Hence his music was almost exclusively 'official'. It is not the least testimony to his character that, though ordered by routine, it bears from first to last the hall-mark of noble inspiration.

But if Bach's Muse was subservient to the situations he filled, the career he followed almost uninterruptedly was his early and deliberate choice. By becoming an organist and Cantor he deserted the traditions of his direct ancestry. His father, grandfather, and great-grandfather were members of secular guilds of musicians, whose duties were not exclusively musical. Had his father lived, he probably would have followed their example. But the premature death of Johann Ambrosius removed an impediment which might have frustrated the career on which his son early set his heart. For, already as a schoolboy Sebastian learnt to regard music as primarily the handmaid of religion, in his own words, 'a harmonious euphony to the glory of God'. It was therefore no sudden impulse that moved him, when little more than twenty, to dedicate himself and his art to God's service. Only once in his purposeful career he divorced himself from it.

Johann Sebastian Bach was born in Thuringian Eisenach *Eisenach* on Saturday, 21 March 1685, the youngest child of *1685-95* Johann Ambrosius Bach and Elisabeth Lämmerhirt. His mother, daughter of an Erfurt furrier, contributed nothing to his genius—she died soon after his ninth birthday. His father, after similar service at Erfurt and Arnstadt, had since 1671 been town's-musician (Stadtmusicus) at Eisenach, where he also chimed the hours and alarmed the community when fire threatened its inflammable roofs. Greatly esteemed by his fellow townsmen, and generally competent in the technique of all the instruments of his craft, he was especially gifted on the violin and viola, for both of which Sebastian was his pupil. At the Eisenach Gymnasium the lad pursued the normal curriculum with precocious success, while he absorbed the romantic associations of the locality. His relative, Johann Christoph Bach, the town's organist, was another potent influence. In after life Sebastian praised him as 'a profound composer', whose motet *I wrestle and pray (Ich lasse dich nicht)* was once supposed to be the younger Master's composition. His brother, Johann Michael Bach, of Gehren, also was a composer of uncommon merit. In their scores, not improbably, Sebastian found his first models of church music. Both brothers were organists, another bond between them and their young relative; and with Johann Michael he was more intimately associated: he married his daughter. It is curious that, neither as organist nor composer, Sebastian drew inspiration from his immediate ancestry.

Sebastian's frequent absences from school at Eisenach

2

betoken a juvenile constitution not robust, and domestic griefs clouded his youthful sky. He lost his mother in 1694, received a stepmother before the year was out, and, just short of three months later (1695), followed his father's coffin to the grave. He was within a few weeks of his tenth birthday. In this crisis of his life good fortune took him to Ohrdruf, where his eldest brother, recently married, was organist. *Ohrdruf* This younger Johann Christoph, fourteen years *1695–1700* Sebastian's senior, was a musician whose competency is declared by the successful careers of his sons, every one of whom received his instruction. He was, moreover, a pupil of Pachelbel, and transmitted to them and to his brother the technique of that Master of the organ. For five impressionable years Sebastian lived under his brother's roof and received his tuition in a branch of their art they alone of their father's sons adopted. At Ohrdruf's school, as at Eisenach, he showed precocious ability, and in its class-rooms imbibed the sturdy faith which fortified him throughout his life; the bias of the school was sternly orthodox. At Ohrdruf, too, his genius for composition began tentatively to declare itself, and he left his brother's roof already drawn to dedicate it to the service of religion.

Sebastian was now fifteen and of an age to find employment. Disinclination for a secular career prevented him from seeking an apprenticeship at Erfurt or elsewhere where his relatives were in office. Providence opportunely opened a door at Lüneburg, far remote from his Thuringian homeland. In the school attached to St. Michael's Church Thuringian voices were in request, and, through the good offices of one of the Ohrdruf masters, Sebastian was summoned to fill a vacancy there. At Easter 1700, after a long and *Lüneburg* venturesome journey, he was enrolled as a discantist *1700–2* of its select choir, in surroundings singularly apt to fit him for his vocation. Neither Eisenach nor Ohrdruf was equipped fully to reveal the potentialities of music as an adjunct to public worship. That instruction he owed to Lüneburg, whose musical resources exceeded those of which he so far had experience. The choir's repertory was wide and

3

eclectic, its library rich in the scores of the masters of polyphony, German, Dutch, Italian, and no less representative of the critical century that stretched back from his own birth to that of Heinrich Schütz. Thus, though his sojourn at Lüneburg was brief, it was of first-rate importance in the enlargement of his experience.

But the organ was his absorbing interest. And here, too, Lüneburg afforded him exceptional opportunities. The famed Georg Böhm, whose music, among others, he had transcribed at Ohrdruf, was organist of St. John's Church. Though a quarter of a century separated their births, Sebastian could not fail to seek the acquaintance of one whom he greatly admired. At Hamburg, too, some thirty miles distant, Böhm's master, the veteran Jan Adam Reinken, was still in service, patriarch of the brilliant school of North German organists. More than once in a summer vacation Sebastian tramped the weary miles to hear one whom in after years his own mastership deeply impressed. Celle, too, was another magnet and instructor. At its ducal court French music and French musicians were the vogue and introduced him to an idiom his own art so greatly enriched later at Cöthen.

Sebastian bade farewell to Lüneburg in the late summer or early autumn of 1702, after more than two years of fruitful experience. Not yet eighteen, fortune so far had befriended him; at no time had he been distant from masters of the instrument on which he desired to excel. Disappointment met him, however, on the threshold of his professional career. In the autumn of 1702 he presented himself at Sangerhausen, a town in Saxony some thirty miles west of Halle, whose Market (St. James's) Church required an organist. He submitted to the customary tests, treated a prescribed melody, accompanied a Choral, extemporized a fugue on a given subject, and so impressed the assessors that, notwithstanding his youth and inexperience, his selection was recommended. Higher authority, however, favoured an older candidate, who received the post in November 1702. Bach's disappointment may have been tempered by the prospect of an imminent and

4

similar opening in his native Thuringia. Meanwhile, being
without means, he needed to earn a livelihood, if not as an
organist, then in some other capacity. Opportunely employment was offered at Weimar, where in April 1703 he *Weimar*
entered the chamber orchestra of Duke Johann *1703*
Ernst, younger brother of the reigning sovereign. His
service there was not prolonged, for on 9 August 1703, as he
had probably anticipated, Arnstadt gave him an organ. His
apprenticeship was over. He was in his nineteenth year.

The restored New (St. Boniface's) Church at Arnstadt, to
which Bach was now attached as organist, had just *Arnstadt*
installed an organ by the Mühlhausen builder *1703–7*
Johann Friedrich Wender. It comprised a Pedal Organ of
five speaking stops, three of 16-foot tone; an upper manual
(Great Organ: Oberwerk) of twelve stops, strong in diapason
tone; and a brilliant lower manual (Brustwerk) of nine stops.
As an organist, Bach never had at his peculiar disposal an
instrument worthy of his skill. But now, for the first time,
an organ was at his exclusive use. His official duties left him
ample leisure to perfect his technique; indeed concentration
upon it eventually displeased his employers, who, though
proud of his talent, deplored his evasion of other tasks which
threatened to curtail his arduous practising. He was induced
to compose a cantata, probably for Easter 1704, but refused
to write another unless he received the assistance of a choirmaster. His thoughts turned often to Lübeck and its organist
Dietrich Buxtehude, whose eminence as composer and player
urgently attracted him. Even in the maturity of his powers
the neighbourhood of a fellow artist always drew him to seek
his acquaintance and, haply, his instruction. But Lübeck was
300 English miles distant! In October 1705, however, he
obtained a month's leave to make the pilgrimage, and prolonged it without sanction till the end of the following January
(1706). He brought back to Arnstadt from his contact with
Buxtehude a newly acquired virtuosity which greatly per-
turbed his congregation. He accompanied the hymns with
unconventional freedom, and set his hearers agape at the
audacity of his improvisations. The Consistory vainly

5

admonished him, and his relations with that body became increasingly uncordial. He had, moreover, outgrown the *Mühl-* meagre opportunities for self-expression the situation *hausen* afforded, and in June 1707 gladly accepted the post of *1707–8* organist in the Church of St. Blaise at Mühlhausen.

Bach remained at Mühlhausen for almost exactly twelve months. He succeeded a musician of eminence, was attached to a church whose beauty contrasted with the unlovely fabric at Arnstadt, and served a community of greater culture and resources. Moreover, he was no longer a bachelor, having taken his Gehren cousin Maria Barbara Bach to wife. Circumstances therefore promised a prolonged residence in Mühlhausen. But his visit to Lübeck had left him no longer resigned to function simply as an organist. He coveted a post which would allow him to dedicate his genius more generously to the service of religion. Mühlhausen impeded his new resolve; for the battle between the Puritan Pietists and orthodox Lutherans raged there with particular fury, and the propriety of elaborate church music was in debate. So, on 25 June 1708, he tendered his resignation. It had been his aim, he complained, to employ music as a vehicle for the exaltation of God's glory, and yet he had encountered vexatious opposition. He had therefore accepted another situation, in which he would be at liberty 'to pursue the object which most concerns me—the betterment of church music'. He begged, and with regret on the part of his employers received, permission to resign.

Bach's new occupation was at Weimar. He described it to *Weimar* his Mühlhausen friends as membership of the Duke's *1708–17* musical establishment (Capelle) and of the more select body of string players who performed in the ducal apartments. But from the first, or after a brief interval, he functioned as Court Organist. The Duke's serious and religious nature promised to support his plans for the improvement of church music, and though, at the outset, he exerted no wider authority than at Arnstadt and Mühlhausen, he correctly anticipated promotion to a post which would effectually enable him to pursue them. Meanwhile his

Weimar period conclusively revealed him as an organist of unrivalled technique, a composer for his instrument of the most inventive genius, an architect of contrapuntal form whose like had not and has not appeared. Nurtured in the traditions of German polyphony, but gifted to endow it with new life, he combined a felicity of melodic utterance with harmonic inventiveness and resource never excelled or equalled. A very large proportion of his masterpieces for the organ were first heard on the instrument incongruously placed in Duke Wilhelm's bizarre chapel. Before he was thirty the foremost German critic dubbed him 'famous', and his profession conceded him a supremacy which only Handel contested. Had he wished, he might in 1713 have succeeded Handel's master, Friedrich Wilhelm Zachau, as organist of the Church of Our Lady at Halle, whose new organ of sixty-three speaking stops strongly attracted him. He seriously entertained the prospect. But his Duke at length placed him in a position to realize the high purpose declared at Mühlhausen six years before. In March 1714 he received appointment as 'Concertmeister', with the obligation to compose cantatas at regular intervals for the ducal chapel.

Preoccupied with the organ, and holding situations which imposed no other routine service upon him, Bach had to this point written little vocal church music. Inadequate material at his disposal made him obstinate in refusing to compose a second cantata at Arnstadt. Impediments of another kind had obstructed him at Mühlhausen. But his visit to Lübeck and experience of its famous performances of church music made him eager to express himself in that form, and the success of his *Gott ist mein König* (No. 71) at Mühlhausen in 1708—its parts were printed at public expense and the work was repeated in 1709 under his direction—fortified the resolve he formed in that year. Prior to his appointment as Concertmeister in March 1714, however, no more than seven church cantatas can be attributed to his pen. But from thenceforward he poured out an astonishing stream, which, with a single intermission, flowed uninterruptedly for thirty years. The bulk of it belongs to Leipzig. But the stream had its

7

source at Weimar, and in that period was decisively grooved in channels from which thereafter it never wandered.

The year 1717 blazed Bach's name throughout Germany and also, ironically, recorded his disgrace. His contest with the Frenchman Marchand at Dresden, unreasonably hailed as a victory for German art, heightened his resentment at his Duke's failure to give him the post of Capellmeister, which had fallen vacant at the close of the previous year (1716). For no other discernible reason, in August 1717, a few weeks before his meeting with Marchand, he accepted the invitation of Prince Leopold of Anhalt-Cöthen to enter his service. For a time the irate Duke refused to release him. But, before the New Year of 1718, with his wife and children, the eldest of them nine years old, Bach opened a new chapter of his career as Capellmeister to the princely Court at Cöthen.

Bach's Cöthen years stand aloof from the main thorough-
Cöthen fare of his life. His active interest in church music
1717–23 was in abeyance. For the Cöthen Court was 're-formed', its chapel a bare vault in which only stern Calvinist psalms were heard. The deprivation of an adequate organ at the zenith of his renown as a player was another disadvantage. Only the exceptional friendliness of his young music-loving master reconciled him to so long an exile from the path he had deliberately chosen, and to it he returned when the Prince's marriage cooled his interest in his Capellmeister's art. Meanwhile, Bach's Cöthen years display another aspect of his embracing genius. The musical establishment he directed consisted of a small body of instrumentalists, whose duty was the entertainment of their sovereign in his apartments. Bach was already versed in the secular music of France and Italy, and his office now required him to express himself in that idiom. He did so with amazing fertility and gusto, in Suites, *Ouvertures*, and other pieces. That the organ was not wholly neglected is evident in the Great G minor Fugue performed at Hamburg in 1720. One or two church cantatas also were added to his store. But his Cöthen music was otherwise exclusively secular and instrumental.

The death of his wife Maria Barbara in July 1720 inclined

8

him to remove from the scene of his loss, and stirred again the ambition she had shared with him at Mühlhausen. Hamburg could have secured him for the vacant organ in St. James's Church there, and the Concertos he dedicated to the Markgraf of Brandenburg in the following year (1721) were probably designed with a view to his migration elsewhere. His second marriage, with Anna Magdalena Wilcken, brought happiness again to his motherless house. But Prince Leopold's subsequent union with one whom Bach disparaged as an 'amusa' diverted him from the interests he had shared with his Capellmeister. Other motives supported Bach's resolution to find employment elsewhere. Cöthen provided inadequate facilities for his children's education: his stubborn Lutheranism would not allow them to attend the more efficient Calvinist school, and a desire to give his elder sons the University education denied to himself may also have moved him. But, above all, the inclination to return to his early and normal associations urged him, and opportunely the death of Johann Kuhnau, Cantor of St. Thomas's School, Leipzig, assisted his inclination. On Quinquagesima Sunday (7 February) 1723 he underwent his trials at Leipzig. More than two months elapsed before he received the appointment, and, after further delay, on Tuesday, 1 June 1723, he was formally inducted. He was a few months beyond his thirty-eighth birthday, and for the rest of his life devoted his ripest genius to the declared purpose of his earlier manhood. *Leipzig 1723–50*

St. Thomas's School, on whose staff Bach functioned as Cantor, was an ancient institution dating from the thirteenth century. Its foundation students (*alumni*), as was the German custom, furnished the civic churches with choirs, receiving in recompense their board and education. The staff comprised a Rector, Conrector, Cantor, and Tertius, who constituted the senior body and taught the foundationers. A similar number of junior masters instructed the non-foundationers, who, as day-boys, were restricted to the lower classes. The *alumni*, Bach's singers, numbered fifty-four, of ages from fourteen to twenty-one, and gave him his immature tenors and basses as well as his sopranos and altos. Divided into separate bodies, they provided choirs for four city churches. In two of them the music was of simple character and employed Bach's least competent singers, whose instruction and direction he left to his prefects. The music which we particularly associate with him—his cantatas, Oratorios, and *Passions*—was heard only in the two principal churches, St. Thomas's and St. Nicholas's, in both of which a generous feast of public worship was spread on Sundays and certain festivals. To only one of the many services, however, the principal one (Hauptgottesdienst), was 'music', as Bach's generation understood the term, admitted. It began at seven in the morning and lasted till about noon. In the course of it a cantata was performed by the choir, organ, and orchestra. At the other services the music was simple and sung to organ accompaniment. At the afternoon service (Vespers) on the three high festivals, however, it was customary to render a Latin *Magnificat* with full orchestral accompaniment, and, on Good Friday, Passion music was performed in similar conditions. For his orchestra Bach drew upon the small company of professional musicians maintained by the municipality, augmented by amateur players drawn from the School and University.

The School had a repertory which successive Cantors had enlarged. But the vogue of new-style music, such as Bach's congregations expected to hear, was comparatively recent, and for its provision he depended in great measure on his own pen. The composition of church music consequently was his absorbing occupation at Leipzig over a period exceeding a quarter of a century. Yet he found time to express himself in other forms. As an organist he had no official status at Leipzig. But he was in much request elsewhere, and some of his greatest music for the instrument belongs to this period. The needs of the University Musical Society (Collegium Musicum), which he conducted for a number of years, and perhaps his obligations as Composer to the Saxon Court at Dresden, account for the orchestral music he wrote in the later years of his Cantorship. To the literature of the keyboard he contributed the four parts of the *Clavierübung* and the second part of the *Well-tempered Clavier* (*Wohltemperirtes Clavier*), and enriched the technics of his art with *The Art of Fugue* (*Die Kunst der Fuge*) and *Musical Offering* (*Musicalisches Opfer*) presented to Frederick the Great.

Apart from the music it inspired, Bach's Leipzig career invites little notice in this outline. His independence of character and insistence upon the prerogatives of his office frequently involved him in conflicts, in which he more than held his own. But his home life was singularly placid and happy, his sons were talented, and only in the last years of his life illness dulled his activities. He died on 28 July 1750 and was buried in the graveyard of St. John's Church, beneath whose altar his ashes now rest.

NOTE

THE fullest narrative of Bach's career is afforded in the present writer's *Bach: a Biography* (Oxford University Press, 1928; new edition 1933). See also his *Bach: the Historical Approach* (Oxf. Univ. Press, New York and London, 1930). The standard works by Parry, Pirro, Schweitzer, and Spitta deal principally with Bach's music.

INSTRUMENTAL
II. THE ORGAN MUSIC

THERE is no musical field in which Bach is not dominant and indispensable. Music emanated from him with apparently equal ease in all its forms, but not, one is sure, with equal satisfaction. Inadequate material, vocal and instrumental, too often alloyed his pleasure, particularly in the rendering of his larger concerted works. On that account, if for no other, he was happiest at the organ, on which his supreme virtuosity completely expressed his design. Of all others it was the medium most responsive to the emotion that swayed him. In its company he soared in free communion with the high intelligences that inspired him. To it he confided his most intimate thoughts, and, could he have foreseen the immortality posterity bestowed on him, he would undoubtedly have associated it with his favourite instrument.

It is therefore surprising that, proportionately to his total output, his organ music is meagre in quantity. The complete tale of his labour is summed in fifty-seven volumes of the Bachgesellschaft edition, of which no more than four (XV, XXV (2), XXXVIII, XL) and a fraction of a fifth (III) contain his organ music. Their contents are displayed in Table I.

The Table records all the organ music accessible to the editors of the Bachgesellschaft volumes. Nor has any important discovery been made since. But it does not represent all that Bach wrote for the instrument. For the extreme paucity of his organ autographs is remarkable, and significant. They are extant for the *Little Book for the Organ* (*Orgelbüchlein*), the six Organ Sonatas, and the Eighteen Choral Preludes. We also have his autograph of four Preludes and Fugues (the 'Great' G major, the 'Great' B minor, the 'Great' C major, the 'Great' E minor), the Fantasia in C minor, two Choral Preludes, and the Canonic Variations on *Vom Himmel hoch*.

But the originals of his other organ compositions are lost. They circulated among his pupils, are known to us in large measure only in their transcriptions of them, and, falling eventually into heedless hands, too often met the fate from which the Violin Solo Sonatas were providentially snatched. The paucity of Bach's autographs, however, is not attributable solely to the ignorance or carelessness of others. He was a severe critic of his work and undoubtedly destroyed much that fell below his maturer standards. The statement is not challenged by the fact that a quantity of his earlier music survives; for it is not extant in his autograph. In his own script we have nothing earlier than the *Little Book for the Organ*, with the possible exception of the 'Great' Prelude and Fugue in G major. His youthful essays had long been extruded from his portfolio and memory.

Bach's perpetually improving technique was instructed by the most laborious and consistent study of accessible models, and his equipment as a composer for the organ advanced with it. At an early age he invited reprimand for his midnight study of the great Masters of the instrument, particularly Dietrich Buxtehude, who represented the traditions of German art at their highest. Celle and its French music revealed to him another idiom, and at Weimar Italy added the last contribution to his self-planned curriculum. Here he studied the scores of Legrenzi, Corelli, Vivaldi, and Albinoni. Here, in the year of his promotion (1714), he copied out the *Fiori musicali* of Frescobaldi, an autograph of 104 pages happily extant at Berlin. From these models he acquired the organized clarity combined with elastic freedom which distinguish him from his German forerunners, whose musical utterance had tended either to looseness of thought or extreme rigidity of form.

In his instrumental, as in his vocal, music Bach expressed himself in the forms convention prescribed. His genius ennobled them all. But the Fugue it trans- *Fugues* formed into an art-form of the utmost expressiveness. Based on the contrapuntal method of vocal polyphony, a Fugue exhibits a rigid thematic subject, first presented in orderly succession in each part, and then treated by the composer with the skill at his command, in such a way as to impose it on the whole movement as its vivid and pervading thought. In Parry's words, the Fugue is 'the highest type of form based on a single thematic nucleus'. For that reason it can easily degenerate into mechanical rigidity. But in Bach's hands, prefixed by the conventional Prelude, or more showy Fantasia or Toccata, the Fugue was endowed with the richest artistic qualities. Modelled with consummate craftsmanship, constructed on themes of genuine melody, and treated with intuitive contrapuntal skill, the Fugue became the most nervous form of self-expression at his command. The processes of his mind, singularly logical and orderly, delighted in a quasi-mathematical problem. But, exhibiting a unique combination of constructional ingenuity and poetic expression, he was able to impose upon the exercise the qualities of pure music. His name and the Fugue are inseparably associated. None before him and none after him has been able to confer on it so consistently the attributes he has taught us to expect and admire. As Beethoven to the Sonata or Haydn to the Quartet, Bach stands to the Fugue as its classic and unrivalled exemplar.

It was at Weimar, in his middle period, that Bach most persistently practised Fugue form. Of the forty-one that are extant nearly thirty (27) are assigned to that period, and among them are six which display his genius at its zenith, and which the admiration of posterity has crowned with the appendant appellation 'the Great': the Fantasia and Fugue in G minor, whose jovial fugal theme Bach borrowed from a Dutch folk-song; the Prelude and Fugue in G major, whose Fugue is an extended version of the opening theme of Cantata No. 21, composed in 1714; the Prelude and Fugue in A minor; the Prelude and Fugue in C minor; the Toccata and Fugue in F major; and the Toccata and Fugue in C major, with its tremendous pedal solo.

To the Weimar decade also belong a few isolated move-*Allabreve* ments in forms Bach did not employ again. The Allabreve in D major is a four-part fugue in the strict *Canzona* style. The Canzona in D minor exhales the same atmosphere as the Allabreve, and, like it, reveals their composer's sympathetic study of Frescobaldi. Both are 'congruous with a solemn and majestic fabric' and calculated 'to stimulate devotional feeling', qualities Forkel especially discerned in Bach's organ style. The Pastorale in F major has the rustic charm and character of its counterpart *Pastorale* in the second Part of the *Christmas Oratorio*. The Trios and Aria in F major we can associate with the maturer Sonatas composed at Leipzig for Bach's eldest son *Trios* Wilhelm Friedemann, of which Forkel declared it 'impossible to overpraise their beauty'. All were designed for a harpsichord with two manuals and pedals, rather than a church organ, and are in the nature of chamber music. Not so the Passacaglia in C minor, in its mighty archi- *Passa-* tecture one of the greatest pieces in the literature of *caglia* the organ. It is built upon a recurring 'thema fugatum' of eight bars:

Bach borrowed the theme from André Raison, a Paris organist in the reign of Louis XIV—a further example of his omnivorous study. On it he constructed a fabric of overpowering grandeur. Set on granite foundations, it rises tier by tier, majestic, proportionate, and capped with glorious brilliance. As an architect of form Bach is unsurpassed and unapproachable.

When Bach left Weimar in 1717 his official career as an organist ended. The Leipzig churches had their own; to none of their instruments he had access, save of another's courtesy. His office was that of choirmaster, his duty to conduct choir, organ, and orchestra in the performance of the weekly cantata. When the cantata was his own work, the organist would naturally permit the composer to displace him in movements whose accompaniment was not fully scored. But otherwise Bach's office neither required him to function as an organist, nor is it likely that he ever claimed to do so.

That he often was heard in St. Thomas's, St. Nicholas's, and St. Paul's is not doubtful, but not officially. Forkel expressly states that, though Bach often gratified visitors by playing to them, he did so always between the hours of service. But his skill as an organist continued to be sought by communities elsewhere, who desired his advice before erecting a new organ, or invited him to display its qualities when completed. If the instrument pleased him, says Forkel, he readily consented to exhibit his talent on it, partly for his own satisfaction, partly for the pleasure of those who were present.

These circumstances throw light on Bach's compositions for the organ at Leipzig. Apart from the Sonatas, which were not composed for the instrument, and five Preludes and Fugues, three of which are ranked among his greatest, all his Leipzig organ compositions are of the kind known as 'Choral Choral- Preludes' (*Choralvorspiele*), that is, short movements vorspiele treating the melody of a congregational hymn. Very nearly half the total sum of Bach's organ music is of this character. In the Bachgesellschaft volumes the whole extant of it fills nearly 800 large quarto pages, of which so many as nearly 300 display the Choral Preludes. What is the explanation of this preponderance?

The explanation is twofold. In the first place, Germany's unrivalled fund of church hymnody was the foundation of German organ technique. This was natural; for its tunes were universally beloved, the hymn-book was the most accessible collection of printed music, and the organ was dedicated exclusively to the same sacred use. Consequently the hymn-book was the organist's earliest lesson-book. So Bach had used it. His first composition was a simple exercise on a hymn-melody, and when the finger of death touched him he was still at work on the same theme.

A second and equally practical reason explains the prominence of the Choral in Bach's organ music. During divine service custom required the organist to 'preambule'. His interludes were not invariably based on a hymn-tune. But at some point he would mark the ecclesiastical season by an appropriate piece of that character, particularly before the seasonal (*de tempore*) hymn, which, at the principal service (*Hauptgottesdienst*), was sung immediately before the Gospel. Bach wrote his Choral Preludes in large measure for this purpose. Hence, his organ music includes preludes on nearly eighty congregational hymn-tunes, simple and elaborate, short and long, suited to every season of the ecclesiastical year.

Of Bach's *Choralvorspiele* there are extant 143 examples, besides four sets of Variations on hymn-melodies. A number of them have come down to us in transcripts by his pupils and others, notably the collection made by Kirnberger of Berlin. The majority, however, reach us in Bach's own autograph, or in copies engraved under his supervision and published with his authority. Unlike the former, they are not haphazard in their contents, but represent four separate collections arranged by Bach himself for a particular purpose. The earliest of them, the *Little Book for the Organ* Orgel- (*Orgelbüchlein*), was compiled in 1717. The other büchlein three—the Schübler Chorals, the Eighteen Preludes, and the Catechism Preludes—belong to Leipzig.

The autograph of the *Little Book for the Organ*, a small quarto in paper boards, bears the following title:

> A Little Book for the Organ, wherein the Beginner may learn to perform Chorals of every Kind and also acquire Skill in the Use of the Pedal, which is treated uniformly obbligato throughout.
>
> To God alone the praise be given
> For what 's herein to man's use written.
>
> Composed by Johann Sebast. Bach, *pro tempore* Capell-meister to His Serene Highness the Prince of Anhalt-Cöthen

Although Bach describes himself as in the service of Prince Leopold of Anhalt-Cöthen, the book was planned at Weimar, was relevant to his duties there, and of no practical use to him thereafter. For that reason it remained incomplete. Upon its ninety-two sheets Bach planned to write 164 Preludes on the melodies of 161 hymns. Actually he composed only 46. They are not inserted consecutively, and upon the intervening leaves he placed only the titles of the melodies he intended to treat there. Thus, the *Little Book for the Organ* contains 46 Choral Preludes and the bare titles of 118 unwritten ones. It forms a condensed Hymnary, based on the hymn-book authorized for use in the Grand Duchy of Weimar in 1713. The latter followed general usage in the arrangement of its contents—First, hymns relative to the Church's seasons and festivals, and, in a second Part, hymns illustrating the various aspects and aspirations of the Christian life. The *Little Book for the Organ* follows the same order. But only the first Part of it, illustrating the Church's seasons, is even approximately complete. Bach planned it to contain 60 Preludes, of which he composed only 36. Part II was designed to include 104, of which only ten actually were written. All are short—no more than ten of the forty-six exceed twenty bars in length—and true examples of the Organ Choral (*Orgelchoral*). They treat the tune in its complete form, uninterrupted by interludes between its several strophes, and decorate it with the composer's richest devices of harmonization and ornament.

Throughout his life the Lutheran hymn-book unfailingly stimulated Bach's interpretative faculty. For his affection for the Choral was not simply a personal inclination. It was in the blood of his nation, a prop of their faith, as essential an adjunct of their devotional equipment as the Bible itself. Indeed, Luther gave Protestant Germany a hymn-book thirty years before he formulated her Creed, and she sang vernacular hymns for generations before she read a vernacular Bible. Both, as M. Pirro writes, 'passed from the inner temple to the outer court, like the reading of Holy Writ', the Bible as 'the book of the family', the hymn-book as 'its musical Breviary'. Thus Bach's treatment of the Chorals in the *Little Book for the Organ* gives an impression of homely intimacy, of a fire-lit interior enclosing a gently-sounding harpsichord. The tunes and their hallowed verses meant so much to him, that his music mirrors the simple faith that sustained him.

A gap of more than twenty years separates the *Orgelbüch-*
Cate- *lein* from Part III of the *Clavierübung*, which Bach
chism engraved and published in 1739. It includes, its
Chorals title-page declares, 'various Preludes [*Vorspiele*] on

18

the Catechism and other Hymns for the Organ'. Bach was never deterred from planning a large design by the objection that it could serve no practical use. In the present case it interested him to employ a number of Luther's hymns to illustrate the Lutheran Catechism. For the purpose he selected six hymns: 1. *Dies sind die heil'gen zehn Gebot'* (The Ten Commandments); 2. *Wir glauben all' an einen Gott* (The Creed); 3. *Vater unser im Himmelreich* (Prayer); 4. *Christ unser Herr zum Jordan kam* (Baptism); 5. *Aus tiefer Noth schrei' ich zu dir* (Penitence); 6. *Jesus Christus, unser Heiland* (Holy Communion). With characteristic reverence he prefaced his exposition of Lutheran dogma with an invocation to the Trinity, for which he chose two more melodies, those of the Litany, *Kyrie, Gott Vater in Ewigkeit*, and the Trinity hymn *Allein Gott in der Höh' sei Ehr'*. Moreover, it pleased him to treat each of the Catechism melodies in two forms, first in a lengthy and elaborate movement, and then in short and simple guise. Perhaps he had in mind to distinguish in this way the longer and shorter Catechisms, for such a design was in keeping with his bent. Each of the three clauses of the *Kyrie* also he duplicates, and the hymn to the Trinity is treated thrice, in homage to the Three Persons. So there are in all twenty-one movements, which exhibit diverse types of treatment and reveal Bach's devotional purpose. Eleven are for the manuals alone, generally in simple counterpoint. The larger movements display Bach's inventiveness and resource, and three are particularly distinguished—the Choral Fantasia on the Lord's Prayer (*Vater unser*), for its scale and harmonic richness; the *Aus tiefer Noth*, which is scored in six parts with double pedal; and the Choral Prelude on the Creed (*Wir glauben all'*), wherein the pedals move with confident strides which have given the movement its popular title, 'The Giant's Fugue'.

The six Schübler Chorals take their name from Johann Georg Schübler, of Zella, near Gotha, to whom Bach *Schübler* sent them to be engraved in or soon after 1746. They *Chorals* are described on the title-page as 'Six Chorals in various forms for an Organ with two Manuals and Pedal'. In fact they were not composed for the instrument, but are arrangements of vocal movements selected from church cantatas composed at Leipzig. We detect no plan or design in their association, and can only infer that, being favourites with him in their original form, Bach desired to give them a wider currency in the only one which would secure it. The first (*Wachet auf, ruft uns die Stimme*) is particularly lovable for its association of the Choral melody with a spacious counter-subject in what Sir Henry Hadow has called 'one of the most beautiful and melodious interplays that even Bach has ever entwined'.

After 1744 Bach appears to have ceased from composing *Eighteen* church cantatas, and devoted himself to the re-*Chorals* vision of his organ music with a view to its publication. When he was seized by his fatal illness he was at work upon a series of movements conveniently known as 'Eighteen Chorals in various forms for an Organ with two Manuals and Pedal.' For the most part they date from his Weimar period, when he was still under the spell of Buxtehude, Pachelbel, and Böhm. But he selected them as worthy of revision, and, as his hand left them, they are, in Mr. Harvey Grace's words, 'as nearly flawless as we have a right to expect from a mere human'. The first fifteen in the manuscript are Bach's holograph. Nos. 16 and 17 are in his son-in-law's handwriting. In No. 18 the manuscript breaks off abruptly in the middle of the twenty-sixth bar. It was Bach's swan-song.

Very early in his career Bach was attracted to the art of *Varia-* varying a given theme and of presenting it with *tions* diverse embroidery. His Goldberg Variations are the classic example of his genius in this form. But it was natural that the hymn-book also should supply him with themes for this purpose, and it did so for almost the first and last of the organ music that he wrote. Among the compositions we associate with his years at Lüneburg are three sets of variations on hymn-tunes—*Christ, der du bist der helle Tag*; *O Gott, du frommer Gott*; and *Sei gegrüsset, Jesu gütig*. Over all of them is an air of ingenuous simplicity. In the closing years of his life he turned again to the same form, a set of

20

five canonic variations upon the Christmas Carol *Vom Himmel hoch, da komm ich her*, published in 1746 and presented in 1747 to the Mizler Society, of which he had just been elected a member. His object was technical—to illustrate the art of canon—and his exposition culminates in a veritable *tour de force* in the final movement. The melody is passed from the treble to the bass, from the bass to the pedals, and from the pedals back again to the treble, while another part is in canon with it at varying intervals. The last five bars are in five parts, and into them Bach contrives to introduce all four lines of the melody, and to decorate them with a profusion of little canons in diminution, which, as Parry remarks humorously, seem to be tumbling over each other in their determination to get into the pattern 'before the inexorable limits of formal proportion shut the door with the final cadence'.

Three things are necessary for the understanding and enjoyment of Bach's Organ Chorals—familiarity with the hymn-tunes he uses, knowledge of the text of the hymns to which they belong, and the key to his musical idiom and language. The first and second are now easily accessible. The third has been fully expounded by Schweitzer and Pirro; unless it is apprehended, much of the significance of Bach's music will be lost, and the range of his thought be missed. Briefly, his language is one of realistic symbolism, and the *Little Book for the Organ* is its pocket lexicon. He was not its originator; for the method was typically German. But it came to maturity with him, and in his usage of it he was consistent from earliest youth to mature old age. As his art developed, his symbols acquired manifold shadings and inflexions. But the master-symbols themselves do not exceed some twenty-five or thirty in number. Some are directional, denoting ascent or descent, height or depth, width, distance, and so forth. The act of hastening or running, and, conversely, the idea of rest or fatigue, are indicated by appropriate symbolic formulas. The moods, again, are distinguished by themes diatonic or chromatic to express joy or sorrow. The thought of laughter, of tumult, of terror, and the forces of nature, the winds, waves, clouds, and thunder have their indicative symbols, which do not vary. Bach was one of the tenderest and most emotional of men, with the eye of a painter and the soul of a poet. But the fact is only fully revealed to those who are at the pains to translate him.

NOTE

THE best and most helpful guide to Bach's organ music is Harvey Grace's *The Organ Works of Bach* (London, 1922). Eaglefield Hull's *Bach's Organ Works* (London, 1929) covers the ground less profitably. Pirro's *Johann Sebastian Bach the Organist*, translated by Wallace Goodrich (New York, 1902), is valuable. Analyses of the organ music are in Schweitzer, vol. i, chaps. 13 and 14, Spitta *passim*, and Parry, chaps. 12 and 14. For the hymns and hymn-tunes of the organ works see the present writer's *Bach's Chorals*, vol. iii (Cambridge, 1921), and *Bach's Four-part Chorals* (Oxford, 1929). The most instructive edition of the *Orgelbüchlein* is published by the Bärenreiter-Verlag, Cassel (ed. Hermann Keller, 1928). Besides the Novello and Augener editions of the organ works, interest attaches to the Schirmer (incomplete) and Peter's editions, from the association of Schweitzer and Widor with the former, and of Karl Straube with the latter.

III. THE CLAVIER AND CEMBALO MUSIC

IN his generation Bach was no less remarkable as a clavier and cembalo (harpsichord) player than as an organist. 'Admired by all who had the good fortune to hear him,' writes Forkel, 'he was the envy of the *virtuosi* of his day.' At his service were three kinds of stringed instrument played at a keyboard: the (1) *clavicembalo*, or, shortly, *cembalo*; (2) *clavichord*, or *clavier*; (3) *Hammerclavier*, or *Fortepiano*. They differed in the mechanism which vibrated their strings, and consequently in their tone; their finger technique was not uniform, and music composed for one was not equally suited to all.

The clavicembalo resembles the modern wing-shaped grand piano in appearance; whence the name 'Flügel' *Cembalo* by which the Germans know it. Its strings are vibrated by quill-points set up on wooden jacks, which pluck or twitch the strings when the keys are depressed. Larger specimens have two manuals and a set of pedals, and their tone quality is controlled by stop-levers, which regulate the number of strings in action.

Externally the clavichord resembles a shallow rectangular box, much smaller than the clavicembalo, easily *Clavi-* transported, and, when in use, resting on its own *chord* supports, or on a table. In Bach's period its range was about five octaves. Its strings are excited by upright brass blades or tangents inserted in the key-levers, which, rising to the strings when the keys are depressed, mark off, and at the same time excite, a length of vibrating string, whose tone the player's finger controls so long as the key is held down. The instrument has no pedals or mechanical device affecting its delicate tone. But, Mr. Dolmetsch observes, 'it possesses a soul, or rather seems to have one, for under the fingers of some gifted player it reflects every shade of the player's feelings as a faithful mirror. Its tone is alive, its notes can be swelled or made to quiver just like a voice swayed by emotion. It can even command those slight vibrations of pitch which in all sensitive instruments are so helpful to expression'—an instrument of very intimate character in a domestic setting.

The Hammerclavier—Beethoven's pianoforte—was im-
Hammer- mature even in Bach's later years. Its strings were
clavier vibrated by hammers, but its mechanism lacked the regulated perfection of the pianoforte. When Bach visited Frederick the Great at Potsdam in 1747 he found in the palace several instruments the king had recently acquired from Gottfried Silbermann, a pioneer in their construction, and on one of them astonished Frederick by his treatment of a theme composed by the monarch. But he had no liking for the instrument, found it coarse in tone, shrill in its upper octaves, and unsuited to his finger technique; he nowhere associates it with his keyboard music.

As between the clavicembalo and clavichord, Forkel asserts
Bach's Bach's preference for the latter: 'Both for practice
usage and intimate use he regarded the clavichord as the better instrument, and preferred it for the expression of his finest thoughts. The clavicembalo, or harpsichord, in his opinion, was incapable of the graded tone obtainable on the clavichord, an instrument of extreme sensitiveness, though feeble in volume.' Forkel, no doubt, is correct in a statement which had the authority of Bach's sons. But it must not be inferred that the clavichord completely displaced its fellow instrument in Bach's usage. For the louder-voiced cembalo universally accompanied concerted music in the seventeenth and eighteenth centuries. Bach's cantata scores, sacred and secular, constantly name it, and for concerted chamber music its use was no less imperative. The weak tone of the clavichord disqualified it for these purposes and reserved it for pure keyboard music. The respective provinces of the two instruments are clearly indicated in Bach's manuscripts. *Das wohltemperirte Clavier* is the title of the instructional exercises he composed for his pupils. For his eldest son he arranged the *Clavier-Büchlein vor Wilhelm Friedemann Bach*. He devised his two-part and three-part Inventions and Symphonies for 'Liebhabern [lovers] des Clavires'. The early

Suites in A minor and E flat major are described in the Autograph as 'pur le Clavesin'. Bach's specification of the clavicembalo is no less precise. The Chromatic Fantasia in D minor is entitled *Fantasia chromatica pro Cimbalo*, as its structure reveals. The Passacaglia in C minor is marked 'Cembalo ossia Organo'. The Italian Concerto, the Partita in B minor, and the Goldberg Variations are allotted to a two-manual clavicembalo. So (with pedal) are the four early Preludes and Fughetta, and much music included in the organ works—the Sonatas, early Choral Variations, Preludes and Fugues. True, some of these are found in a publication bearing the title *Clavierübung* (*Diversions for the Clavier*). But Bach borrowed the word from his predecessor Kuhnau with a purpose, and it has so loose a connotation that in Part III it covers the Catechism Preludes, which are definitely 'vor die Orgel'. Thus Bach's preference for the clavichord, which Forkel correctly asserts, did not exclude the other instrument from uses for which it was better equipped. The clavier was the more responsive to his touch and more sensitively interpreted his emotions. But in his keyboard music of larger design or more showy intention, as in his concerted music, the clavicembalo better fulfilled his purpose.

As Table II reveals, Bach's keyboard music is associated with every period of his active career. Besides the larger works, it exhibits a considerable number of detached pieces which represent his assiduous self-discipline, and, at the same time, afforded him agreeable relaxation from the major tasks which constantly preoccupied him. In his early years a small number of extant pieces—Fantasias, Fugues, Preludes, Toccatas, a couple of Capriccios, and a Sonata in D major— reveal his maturing genius. The Capriccio in B flat *Capric-* is specially notable, a vivid piece of programme *cios* music, which Parry does not hesitate to call 'the most dexterous piece of work of the kind that had ever appeared in the world up to that time'. It was written at Arnstadt, about 1704, to mark the departure of the composer's brother, Johann Jakob, who was entering the Swedish service as an oboist. We hear the traveller's friends dissuading him from

25

the hazardous journey. In a short fugal movement they depict the dangers ahead. Then (*Adagissimo*) we hear their lamentations, till the postilion's horn sounds, and off goes the coach to a brisk and entertaining fugue! The Capriccio in E major, less interesting musically, is equally so as a token of fraternal regard. For the piece is inscribed 'in honorem Johann Christoph Bacchii', the Ohrdruf brother to whom Bach owed his first lessons on the keyboard. Probably it was composed soon after his return from North Germany to demonstrate his progress along a path on which his brother was his earliest guide. It consists of a single fugal movement on a somewhat uninteresting theme. But it sufficiently displays the youthful composer's deftness in the treatment of his material to please the eye for whose observation it was intended. The Sonata in D major, like the Capriccio in B flat, reveals the influence of Johann Kuhnau, whom Bach succeeded twenty years later at Leipzig, and whose Biblical Sonatas, recently (1700) published, were now his model. For the moment their descriptive method attracted him: the last movement of the Sonata is on a subject quaintly indicated as 'A theme in imitation of a clucking hen'!

At Weimar Bach was preoccupied with the organ and, latterly, with the composition of church cantatas. Consequently the tale of his keyboard music is meagre—a few arrangements, notably the Violin Concertos by Vivaldi and others, a couple of Fantasias, five Fugues, some early Suites, and the *Aria variata* in A minor. They all evidence the Italian influences in which at this period Bach was steeping himself. Vivaldi attracted him both as a violinist and composer. Only seven of the adapted Concertos, however, are by him: three of them were composed by the talented young Duke Johann Ernst of Weimar. Two of the Fugues, also, are on themes borrowed from the Italian Tommaso Albinoni. The Aria in

A minor, again, is 'variata alla maniera italiana', on a tender theme, which, in Spitta's words, 'seems to wander *Aria* like a shade through the variations, but blossoms out *variata* again in the full beauty of intoxicating harmony in the last'. But Weimar inspired no music for clavier or cembalo to equal the organ masterpieces there brought to birth. To match them Bach's genius awaited the next step in his career.

A double duty rested on Bach at Cöthen. The Suites we owe to his function as Capellmeister. With other works of large design, of which the Chromatic Fantasia and the Toccatas in C minor and F sharp minor are most noteworthy, they represent the response of his official Muse. But circumstances imposed on him a more domestic duty. In November 1719 his eldest son, Wilhelm Friedemann, kept his ninth birthday. Bach at that age had received his first lesson on the clavier, and he introduced his children to it at the same period. His youngest son's ninth year was marked by the composition of the second Part of *The Well-tempered Clavier* at Leipzig. And now, at Cöthen, on 22 January 1720, his eldest son received his first lesson in an exercise-book prepared with meticulous care. For the occasion was one of solemnity to a father who destined his son for his own profession, and that profession semi-sacred. First in his *Clavier-Büchlein* Friedemann found explanations *Friede-* of the clefs and ornaments—the trill, mordent, *mann's* cadence, and so forth. Next, under the reverent *Clavier-* ascription 'In the Name of Jesus', came his first *Büchlein* finger exercise:

Among the exercises that follow are fifteen two-part pieces (*Praeambulum*) arranged in key-sequence; fourteen three-part pieces (*Fantasia*) similarly marshalled; eleven Preludes (*Praeludium*) in order of tonality; six more, not entered consecutively, but fitted into the key-plan of the whole and entitled *Praeludium* or *Praeambulum*; and a Minuet-Trio, added to a Partita by another composer. The fifteen two-part and fourteen three-part pieces are known to us in another autograph as the *Inventions and Symphonies*; the eleven Pre-ludes are found also in *The Well-tempered Clavier*; and the six scattered Preludes and Preambules and Minuet-Trio are among the *Twelve Little Preludes*. Along with the *Six Preludes for Beginners* these titles name the 'Clavier School' on which Bach brought up his sons and pupils.

Inventions and Symphonies

As a complete and separate collection, the Inventions and Symphonies come to us in an autograph written in 1723 on the eve of Bach's migration to Leipzig. Its prefatory title declares the uses it was designed to serve:

A faithful Guide, in which Lovers of the Clavichord, particularly such as are truly anxious to learn, may find a clear System for clean playing in two Parts, and for correct and finished playing in three; and, at the same time, a Model on which they may learn how to form Inventions and develop them, and, above all, acquire a *cantabile* Style in their playing, and receive an incentive and taste for Composition.

Bach's choice of the uncommon definition 'Invention' affords another example of his familiarity with contemporary Italian music. The Bachgesellschaft edition prints four 'Inventions' extant in his autograph, which were believed to be his compositions. In fact they are by Francesco Antonio Bonparti, who wrote them when Bach was in service at Weimar. They do not resemble his own genuine Inventions. But he was grateful for the word, and deemed it more applicable to his contrapuntal two-part pieces than the title he had given them in Friedemann's book. For Forkel correctly defined Bach's Invention as 'a musical theme so constructed that by imitation and inversion it can provide the material for an entire movement'. He commended the fifteen as 'invaluable exercises for the fingers and hands, and sound

28

models of taste'. Such was their primary purpose. But they are far removed from the dull literature of the schoolroom. For here, as in all his instructional music, Bach had an ulterior purpose, which his prefatory title reveals. His intention was to shape the pupil's artistic sense, and to stimulate his latent faculties as a composer, a motive that seems extravagant till we remember that his students were embryo Cantors and organists, and that in his eyes music was the most worthy homage man could offer to his Maker. He aimed also to inculcate the *cantabile* style, possible on the clavier alone, but then too little practised. Both Inventions and Symphonies are arranged in the 1723 autograph in the ascending order of the scale, from C major to B minor. But there is a definite relation of mood or material between each Invention and its corresponding Symphony: indeed, in another manuscript each pair is brought together in this way. All are perfect miniatures in form and content, as satisfying to the accomplished player as they are instructive to the youngest. 'Only an infinitely fertile mind', Schweitzer remarks with truth, 'could venture to write thirty little pieces of the same style and the same compass, and, without the least effort, make each of them absolutely different from the rest. In face of this inconceivable fertility it seems almost a superfluous question to ask whether any other of the great composers has had an inventive faculty so infinite as Bach's.'

Unlike the Inventions and Symphonies, Bach's instructional Preludes reach us in haphazard association. *Little* Seven of them are found in Friedemann's *Clavier- Preludes Büchlein*—Nos. 1, 4, 5, 8, 9, 10, 11 of the *Twelve*—and five more—Nos. 2, 3, 6, 7, 12 of the *Twelve*—in the manuscripts of Johann Peter Kellner (1705–72), who was personally known to Bach, but not his pupil. These are printed under a single title in the Bachgesellschaft edition, and are universally styled the *Twelve Little Preludes*. The other six were first published by Forkel, and the title he gave them—*Six Preludes for Beginners*—has been generally adopted. Consequently, neither set exhibits a completely ordered plan. In the larger one the keys of E major, G major, A major, and B minor are not illustrated, and those in C major, D minor, F major, and G minor are duplicated. In the smaller, no examples are provided for the keys above E. But all are fresh and fragrant, especially the delicate Minuet-Trio Bach added to J. G. Stöltzel's Partita in his son's *Little Book*.

The crown and glory of Bach's instructional music is *The* *Well-tempered Clavier*, which, in Spitta's opinion, *Well- tempered* 'reflects the whole of the Cöthen period of Bach's *Clavier I* life, with its peace and contemplation, its deep and solemn self-collectedness'. The Berlin autograph bears the title:

The well-tempered Clavier; or, Preludes and Fugues on every Tone and Semitone, with the major third Ut, Re, Mi, and minor third Re, Mi, Fa. For the Use and Profit of young Musicians anxious to learn, and as a Pastime for others already expert in the Art. Composed and put forth by Johann Sebastian Bach, presently Capellmeister and Director of Chamber-Music at the princely Court of Anhalt-Cöthen. Anno 1722.

At Leipzig, in later years, Bach played the whole work through thrice to his pupil Heinrich Nikolaus Gerber, who probably then received the story of its inception published many years later by Gerber's son. As an illustration of Bach's invariable independence of the keyboard when composing, the latter records that *The Well-tempered Clavier* was written when Bach was idle in a spot lacking musical instruments of every kind. The story is not improbable. Bach was wont to accompany Prince Leopold on his journeys, and returned from one of them in 1720 to find his wife dead, a tragic close to a journey in whose course *The Well-tempered Clavier* may have been compiled. He appears to have solaced an earlier period of confinement by arranging *The Little Book for the Organ*. And his independence of the keyboard is otherwise authenticated. Forkel remarks on his derision of 'Harpsichord Riders', 'Finger Composers', whose uninspired hands ran up and down the keyboard in hope to strike an idea worth capturing.

Bach deliberately chose the title he prefixed to the twenty-four Preludes and Fugues. It registered his approval of an innovation in the European scales system, without which the avenues modern music has since explored must have remained closed. Bach's purpose was to demonstrate the practicability of 'equal temperament' by providing pieces in every key, major and minor, for the clavier tuned on that principle. The controversy was ancient. Composers of old-style music, content with a few keys—in general such as had not more than three sharps or flats in their signature—were willing to sacrifice all others to secure theoretical correctness of intonation in the few. The more progressive realized the limitations this 'mean-tone' or 'unequal temperament' imposed upon their art: it rendered modulation outside the preferred scales impossible. They therefore advocated the method of tuning known as 'equal temperament', which proposed to make all the semitones in the scale equal. Hence, each octave would be divided into twelve equal semitones; every scale, instead of a few, would be approximately correct; and the bar to free modulation would be removed. The twelve-semitoned scale has become universal, and by practical demonstration Bach's *Well-tempered Clavier* assisted to establish it.

There is no doubt that, besides the public service the twenty-four Preludes and Fugues were designed to fulfil, Bach intended them for his children's instruction. He made copies of them for Friedemann and Carl Philipp Emanuel. And twenty-two years later (1744), when his youngest son Johann Christian was starting on the road they formerly had traversed, he compiled another set of twenty-four on the same principle, but not under the same title. For the controversy over temperament was no longer active, and further propaganda was not required. Bach apparently entitled the set 'Twenty-four new Preludes and Fugues', forming, with the original collection, the immortal '48'. There are other indications of his aloofness from the circumstances which produced the earlier set. It is observed by Professor Tovey that the later twenty-four are less evidently written in terms of the clavichord than the first series, with which instrument their title definitely associates them. Further, Mr. Fuller-

Maitland remarks that the second set is less obviously instructional; Bach was thinking less of 'young Musicians anxious to learn' than of 'others already expert in the Art'. That he incorporated in both sets pieces of earlier date than the autographs is immaterial. They hold their place worthily in a galaxy of exceptional lustre. 'Both Parts', Forkel boasted sixty years after the appearance of the second, 'contain artistic treasures not to be found outside Germany.' Nor has their like been seen since Forkel proclaimed Bach's grandeur to his countrymen. Their technical skill is matchless, but so controlled that they chiefly stir us as the noble diction of great literature, the vehicle of lofty thought.

As Capellmeister, Bach's Cöthen keyboard music was almost exclusively in Suite form. Occasionally he displayed his virtuosity as a player in movements of more brilliant texture—the Chromatic Fantasia and Fugue, the Fantasia and Fugue in A minor, and the Toccatas in F sharp minor and C minor. But, in general, he provided music agreeable to the general taste. And of all forms of chamber music the Suite was the most popular, whether for solo instruments or orchestral *ensemble*.

The Suite comprises a few—generally seven or eight— short movements bearing the name, and in the distinctive rhythm, of characteristic national dances. *Suites* The universal employment of a French designation for this, the earliest, cyclic art-form declares its original source, and Bach most usually employed it. But the seven he wrote at Leipzig bear the title 'Partita', and occasionally the term 'Sonata'—as in those for Solo Violin and Solo Violoncello— covers a composition of similar character. 'Ouverture', again, is the alternative name for the orchestral Suites.

Under whatever title it passed, the Suite comprehended a string of dance measures of international currency and diversity. Their contrasts, no doubt, originated the idea of stringing them together, and at first no rigid principle selected those admitted. But, long before Bach was born, four established a preferential claim for inclusion—the *Allemande*, *Courante* (or *Coranto*), *Sarabande*, and *Gigue* (or *Jig*); while the *Gavotte, Bourrée,* and *Minuet* were also popular. The Allemande expressed the solemn nature of the German, the Courante the fervid temperament of the Italian, the Sarabande the courtly dignity of Spain, the Gigue the robust jollity of the Englishman, and the Minuet or Gavotte the refined gaiety of France. Consequently, the Suite was well adapted to the purposes it served: it was varied in its contents, melodious, neither too long to be irksome, nor too short to appear trivial. Only in one particular it was monotonous: convention required all its movements to be pitched in the same key, a blemish of which its public was less conscious than our own. Only in the English Suites, the detached Suite in E flat, and the Partita (or French Ouverture) in B minor, is the persisting key sequence interrupted. In these eight instances usually the penultimate movement, or another, is in two divisions, one of which changes to the relative major or minor. Throughout the whole twenty-six Bach's inclination to satisfy the champions of unequal temperament is evident. The last of the French Suites is in E major: otherwise their signatures do not exceed three sharps or flats. All of them are suited to the harpsichord rather than the clavichord, for they invite the tonal contrasts which only the former could afford.

Fourteen of the nineteen keyboard Suites belong to Bach's Cöthen period. One is unfinished. Another (in B flat) is not certainly authenticated. The other twelve have come to us in two sets of six, distinguished popularly as the 'French' and 'English'. The titles lack the sanction of Bach's authority, but were evidently used by his sons. Forkel, in intimate touch with both of them, explains that the 'French Suites' were so called 'because they are written in the French style', and that the others were known as the 'English Suites' 'because the composer wrote them for an Englishman of rank'. Of both sets autographs have survived. The French Suites are found, though imperfect, in Anna Magdalena Bach's earlier *Note-book,* which places their composition before 1722; and on an early manuscript of the English set the inscription 'composed for the English' (*fait pour les Anglois*) heads the

33

first Suite. No reason is apparent why the French set should be particularly distinguished by the name: their measures are not characteristically French. Nor is Forkel's statement regarding the English Suites convincing. The Prelude of the first introduces a theme by Charles Dieupart, a popular French harpsichordist in London during Bach's early manhood. But the coincidence, though interesting, does not explain the words 'composed for the English'. The conjecture that the Suite was written for the English public is, of course, untenable. The inscription must therefore refer to particular Englishmen, and, if the date of the set is accurately placed, to visitors at Cöthen. Between the Anglo-Hanoverian Court and the petty German principalities conventions were not infrequent, and the 'old Dessauer', Prince Leopold of Anhalt-Dessau, Marlborough's sometime colleague, was still living. A military Commission perhaps visited Cöthen, was entertained by the Prince, and received from his Capellmeister the compliment of a composition specially dedicated. To such an audience the composer would wish to display his familiarity with English practice by borrowing a theme from London, and also by framing the Suite—and subsequently the remaining five of the set—in a distinctively English form. For they differ from the French set in the fact that each is prefaced by an elaborate Prelude, like those of Henry Purcell and his precursors.

Bach's keyboard Suites contain not far short of two hundred movements. They exhibit extraordinary fertility of invention, vivid imaginative power, and complete technical mastery of the forms they employ. Some are of poignant beauty—the Sarabandes of the first, fifth, and sixth French Suites, and, above all, of the second English Suite. But their pervading tone is of happy humour and exuberant good nature, especially the fifth of the French and fourth of the English. It has been suggested that Bach was a disgruntled revolutionary, beating his wings with angry futility against the circumstances which confined him. The picture is out of drawing. He was an incorrigible optimist, and so his Suites proclaim him.

The secular character of his Cöthen duties afforded Bach opportunity and incentive to cultivate the Flügel, *Finger-* which most closely approached the organ in its *ing* technique. Forkel particularly records his meticulous care of his instrument. No hands but his own were suffered to tune it or his clavichord, an operation in which he was so skilful that he accomplished it in a quarter of an hour. He tuned the strings always to equal temperament, and consequently used the whole twenty-four scales, major and minor. But the finger technique of his early manhood was inadequate for the complete expression of his complex harmonies and brilliant passage work. Equal temperament, also, brought the neglected black notes on the keyboard into action, and, along with the new forms in which music was expressing itself, insistently demanded a more adequate keyboard technique. As his abnormal power developed, Bach was conscious of the restraint imposed upon him, and, before his meeting with Marchand in 1717, jettisoned the accepted system of fingering, which found no use for the thumb or little finger, and little for the first. Bach, on the contrary, gave the thumb regular duty in the scale and compelled the idle little finger to pull its weight.

These changes had important consequences. The thumb having become their active partner, the fingers could no longer lie flat and extended over the keyboard, but needed to withdraw their extremities in order to accommodate themselves to its shorter length. Consequently, they assumed a curved shape, their tips poised above the keys, giving the player the utmost facility for rapid passages, and also adapted to the *cantabile* or *legato* style Bach impressed upon his pupils as proper to the harpsichord no less than to the organ. His hands, like Handel's, maintained their bunched shape even in the most intricate passages, and his fingers were so controlled that they appeared hardly to move.

Prince Leopold was an amateur musician for whose abilities Bach had sincere respect. The Prince, on his side, was attracted to his Capellmeister as much by his executive powers as by his felicity as a composer, which, in fact, before 1718 had been expended on forms to which a Calvinist Court

35

was indifferent. There is every reason, therefore, to suppose that the brilliant keyboard 'show-pieces' composed at Cöthen were performed by Bach himself at the *soirées* which periodically entertained the princely audience in the Ludwigsbau of the Schloss. Prominent among them is the Chromatic Fantasia and Fugue in D minor. From the first it was one of Bach's most popular compositions; Forkel, who received a copy of it from Friedemann Bach, observed truly that, 'if performed even tolerably, it appeals to the most ignorant hearer'. In the Fantasia, which has the brilliance of the Great Fantasia in G minor for the organ, Bach adventures daring feats of modulation. The general effect, as Spitta observes, is of 'an emotional *scena*', in which the chromatic fugue pulses forward in 'a mighty demoniacal rush'. Worthily Forkel's copy bore the inscription, 'Glorious for all time!'

Fantasias

The Fantasia in A minor is not less bold and spirited, and its Fugue—the longest Bach ever wrote (198 bars!)—exhibits his boundless resource. Built on a spirited theme in semi-quavers, it spins its course in a whirling *perpetuum mobile*. The Toccatas in F sharp minor and C minor complete this quartet of Cöthen exhibition pieces. Sir Hubert Parry declares the Toccata 'a branch of art which has been more piteously discredited than any in its whole range, save and except the operatic aria'. These two exhibit the form, and Bach's handling of it, at the zenith. In that in F sharp, after a bravura introduction, we pass to a nobly expressive interlude (*Adagio*), after which, in Spitta's graphic words, 'it is as though spirits innumerable were let loose, whispering, laughing, dancing up and down, teasing or catching each other, gliding calmly and smoothly on a translucent stream, wreathed together into strange and shadowy forms; then suddenly the phantoms have vanished, and the hours of existence are passing as in everyday life, when the former turmoil begins afresh'. The C minor also, opening stormily, passes to a meditative *Adagio*, from which a strong fugal theme emerges, 'a proud and handsome youth, swimming on the full tide of life, in delightful consciousness of his strength'.

Bach's appointment to Leipzig in 1723, and his consequent preoccupation with church music, immediately diverted him from the peculiar activities of his Cöthen service. Circumstances, however, led him to resume them, though intermittently. His predecessor Kuhnau's reputation so largely rested on his keyboard compositions, and official Leipzig's early attitude towards himself was so coldly critical, that Bach was moved to challenge Kuhnau in his own field. The latter had published a set of Partitas (*Partien*) under the title *Neue Clavir-Übung*, and other works, which set him at a bound in the front rank of composers for the instrument. The considerations that guided Bach's selection of the compositions he engraved are often obscure. *Clavier-übung I* But there is no doubt that the deliberate intention to put himself in competition with Kuhnau's reputation led him in 1726 to issue the first instalment of what he published five years later as his 'Opus I'. Borrowing Kuhnau's title, he announced it as:

> Clavier Diversions: comprising Preludes, Allemandes, Courantes, Sarabandes, Gigues, Minuets, and other Galantries. Composed for the Delectation of Music Lovers by Johann Sebastian Bach. . . . Partita I. Published by the Composer.

Each succeeding year he published another Partita, and in 1731 issued the six together as 'Part I' of his *Clavier Diversions*. In texture they are lighter than the English Suites, and their general character indicates that Bach was less concerned to demonstrate his mature technique than to satisfy the public taste. As in the Cöthen Suites, an Allemande, Courante, and Sarabande are included in all, and a Gigue ends every one but the second. Like the English Suites, the Allemande in each is preceded by an introductory movement, but distinct in name and design—*Praeludium, Sinfonia, Fantasia, Ouverture, Praeambulum,* and *Toccata*. The 'Galanterien' include some which find no place in the Cöthen compositions—a Rondeau and Capriccio in the second Partita, a Burlesca and Scherzo in the third. That some or all may have been in Bach's portfolio at Cöthen is suggested by the fact that the

37

third and Sixth Partita are found in Anna Magdalena Bach's second *Note-book*, which puts back their composition at least to the year preceding the publication of the first. But the material point is that Bach selected them for a purpose, and that the public voice confirmed his choice. Forkel records that they attracted much notice: 'Such compositions for the clavier had not been seen or heard before, and anyone who could play them was sure of being applauded, so brilliant, agreeable, expressive, and original are they.' Spitta's conjecture that Bach published them as distinctive types of the German Suite in contrast with his English and French sets is not tenable.

Four years later (1735) Bach published Part II of his *Clavier Diversions*, containing two compositions for the two-manual cembalo—a seventh Partita (in B minor) and a Concerto in F major. His title-page announced the former as 'an Ouverture in the French style', and the Concerto as 'after the Italian manner'. He issued the two works together because in each he was attempting to adapt an orchestral form to the technique of the cembalo, an experiment he did not repeat. That being his purpose, the Partita lacks the customary Allemande, a movement nowhere admitted to his orchestral Suites; the normal Allemande-Courante-Sarabande sequence is not observed, and the number of 'Galanterien' is unusually large—two Gavottes, two Passepieds, two Bourrées, and, following the Gigue, an Echo.

Clavier-übung II

French Ouverture

Like the Partita, the Italian Concerto is Bach's only work of the kind for the cembalo. It is in three movements, the second and third of which are marked *Andante* and *Presto* respectively, while the first, though unmarked, is evidently a brisk *Allegro*. Bach found the opening theme of the *Allegro* in a work by Georg Muffat (d. 1704), a musician of Scottish origin, Capellmeister to the Bishop of Passau. But its treatment reveals his own individual mastery and greatly enhanced his reputation. Johann Adolf Scheibe, not always a friendly critic, praised it as 'provoking the envy and emulation' of other German composers, and as the object of 'vain imitation

Italian Concerto

by those of foreign countries'. Spitta distinguishes it as the classical precursor of the modern pianoforte Sonata.

Part III of *Clavier Diversions* appeared in 1739. Early in that year, Johann Elias Bach, then residing in the *Clavier-* Cantor's house, informed a correspondent that his *übung III* cousin had completed pieces 'eminently suited to the organ', and in the following September they were on sale for three thalers. The publication was in the nature of a miscellany: it includes, besides the Catechism Preludes and other movements for the organ, four two-part Duets—in E minor, F major, G major, and A minor. On a larger scale they are examples of the movements Bach styled 'Inventions' at Cöthen. His inclusion of them in incongruous association here must be attributed to his wish to demonstrate the fuller capabilities of this novel form, his own invention. Therein they amply succeeded. Otherwise, they are a further indication of an inclination in his last years to develop to their utmost the technical possibilities of the forms he employed.

It is noteworthy that uniform intervals of four years separated the publication of the first three Parts of *Clavier-* the *Clavier Diversions*. Probably, therefore, the *übung IV* fourth and last, usually dated 'about 1742', appeared in 1743. The reasons for a regulated interval are not apparent. The third, however, was certainly intended for the annual Easter Fair, when Leipzig was thronged with visitors. The other Parts probably appeared at the same period. At these seasons Kuhnau was in the habit of conducting concerts, and Bach may have followed the tradition. If so, his *Diversions* were probably introduced by himself to a cosmopolitan audience. Part IV, however, was composed for a domestic platform. It consists of a single work, described as 'An Aria with several Variations, for a two-manual clavicembalo'. Forkel *Goldberg* tells the story of its inception as he received it from *Variations* Bach's sons. Among the most prominent members of the diplomatic circle at the Dresden Court was the Russian Envoy, Carl Freiherr von Kayserling. Bach was under obligation to him, had received the patent of his appointment

39

as Court Composer from him in 1736, and probably was in some degree indebted to him for the distinction. He suffered from insomnia, and so required his house musician, Johann Theophilus Goldberg, to sleep in a room adjoining his own, in readiness to play to him when he was wakeful. On the occasion of one of his frequent visits to Leipzig he invited Bach to compose some keyboard music, soothing and cheerful, to relieve the tedium of sleepless nights. He offered a handsome fee, and Bach accepted the commission. Though the form had never attracted him, he judged a set of variations best adapted to the circumstances he was invited to alleviate, and composed the work which has immortalized Goldberg by its association with him.

Searching for a theme on which to build, Bach found in his wife's second (1725) *Note-book* a Sarabande in G major, whose ground-bass attracted him:

Bach treats this theme in Passacaglia style, making it the basis of the thirty variations. Determined to give his patron the most generous and differing medicine for his insomnia, he invented a surprisingly varied series of movements. Ten of the variations are for both manuals, in three the use of two is optional, in fifteen a single keyboard is prescribed, and two lack a specific indication. The subject is treated in canon at every interval, from the unison (No. 3) to the ninth (No. 27). In one movement the theme is cast in the form of a Fughetta (No. 10). Another (No. 16) is planned as an Ouverture. No. 25 is an *Adagio* in Sonata style, No. 26 a Sarabande, and the last of all (No. 30) a Quodlibet, in which, above the ground theme, two popular songs are worked out together:

(a)

So long have I been part-ed from thee; Re-turn, re-turn, re-turn!
Ich bin so lang nicht bei dir ge - west; Ruck her, ruck her, ruck her!

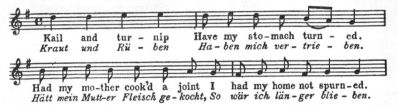

Kail and tur - nip Have my sto-mach turn - ed.
Kraut und Rü - ben Ha- ben mich ver - trie - ben.

Had my mo-ther cook'd a joint I had my home not spurn-ed.
Hätt mein Mutt-er Fleisch ge- kocht, So wär ich län-ger blie - ben.

Forkel declared the work worth at least a thousand times the fee Bach received for it. Sir Hubert Parry, endorsing his enthusiasm, extols it as 'among the few greatest examples of this form of art in existence'.

Apart from the *Clavier Diversions* and the second twenty-four Preludes and Fugues of *The Well-tempered Clavier*, Bach wrote little keyboard music at Leipzig—a Fantasia in C minor, Fantasia and Fugue in A minor, Prelude and Fugue in E flat, and the Suites in C minor and E minor. The C minor Fantasia, composed about 1738, *Leipzig Fantasias* exhibits the Neapolitan clavier style, a characteristic of which was the crossing of the hands. Spitta regards it as the precursor of Carl Philipp Emanuel Bach's Sonata form. Particular interest attaches to the Suites and Prelude and Fugue. They conform in construction with other examples which have been reviewed. But they are unique in a characteristic common to them all. Bach's autograph of *Lute* the Prelude and Fugue prescribes it alternatively *music* for the lute. Manuscripts of the two Suites assert a similar association. There is good evidence that Bach played the lute and instructed his pupils in the technique of the instrument. But there is nothing to indicate that he wrote for it before he came to Leipzig. Hence, if they were composed originally for the lute, the three compositions must be attributed to that period. If, on the other hand, they were adapted to it, the Suites, in their original form, probably were written at Cöthen. An E major Suite, which exists also as the third Partita for Solo Violin, is in the same category, though there is less reason to regard it as a lute composition. Bach, in fact, wrote or adapted very little music for the lute. Only two pieces, besides those already named, can be

41

associated with it—the third of the *Twelve Little Preludes* (in C minor) and the Fugue of the organ Prelude and Fugue in D minor.

NOTE

BACH'S keyboard music is discussed in Spitta *passim*; Schweitzer, i, chap. 15; Parry, chaps. 12–14. For the Suites and Partitas Fuller-Maitland's *Bach's Keyboard Suites* ('The Musical Pilgrim', 1925) is very helpful. Besides the editions of *The Well-tempered Clavier* named in the Table, mention must be made of the Novello text (ed. Harold Brooke), and, especially, the edition prepared for the Associated Board of the R.A.M. and R.C.M. by Professor Tovey and fingered by Harold Samuel. For a concise analysis of each of the '48' see Fuller-Maitland's *The '48': Bach's Wohltemperirtes Clavier* ('The Musical Pilgrim': 2 bks., second impression, 1928). The Peters edition prints Bach's keyboard music in 23 books.

IV. THE CHAMBER MUSIC

BEFORE the Public Concert was instituted, a development
barely within Bach's experience, music, other than domestic,
was composed mainly for the church, the stage, and the *salons*
of princely or aristocratic patrons. Chamber music furnished
the last of these platforms, and, though its forms were not constant, they included those inappropriate to the other audiences.

In whatever form it was composed, the chamber music of
Bach's period was based on principles rejected by   *The*
the later practice of Haydn and Mozart. Modern *Continuo*
chamber music is a co-partnery of equal instrumental parts,
whose *ensemble* completely achieves the composer's harmonic
scheme. Bach's chamber music, and the traditions which it
acknowledged, conflict with this scheme in essential particu-
lars. In the first place, whatever the combination of instruments, and in whichever form, Sonata or Concerto, the
harmonic background is not fully unfolded by the real parts,
but is completed by an auxiliary, denominated the *continuo*,
or *basso continuo*, or *figured bass*, or *thorough bass*, entrusted
to a player who 'fills in' from the skeleton part before him.
Moreover, this auxiliary part is performed by a keyboard
instrument—the cembalo—capable of 4-foot and 16-foot
doublings. This fact, along with its quality of extemporization,
sets the continuo radically apart from the instrumental voices
with which it associates, and destroys the instrumental
equality which is the characteristic of modern chamber music.

The continuo system developed during the seventeenth
century, reached its classic period in the scores of Bach and
Handel, and was rejected by the revolution accomplished by
Haydn in the generation that followed their deaths. Primarily
the continuo is the 'Fundamento', the bass support of the
musical structure. But, for reasons to be stated, seventeenth-
and eighteenth-century composers figured it with numerals,
in a sort of tablature. These numerals measured the distance
of a desired sound from the bass note below which they were
written, and were arranged in descending order of magnitude,
the largest at the top: e.g. $\begin{smallmatrix} 6 & 7 & 6 & 4 & 4 & 6 & 7 \\ 4, & 3, & 5, & 3, & 2, & 4, & 5, \\ & & & & 2 & & \sharp \end{smallmatrix}$ &c.

But the player was not bound to space his chord in exact conformity with this numerical arrangement, and the notes indicated by the figuring were deemed to be in accordance with the key unless accompanied, or, sometimes, in the case of the figure 3, replaced by a ♯, ♭, or ♮. Associated with the written notes of the continuo, these symbols instructed the player to provide particular harmonies, and, subject to conventions with which he was familiar, he extemporized an accompaniment on the figured bass in accordance with them.

This method came into vogue partly as the consequence of the monodic revolution accomplished at the beginning of the seventeenth century, which substituted a new musical form for the pure vocal polyphony of Palestrina and the Golden Age, and with it created a problem for composers. The monodists, as the word implies, invented the recitative for a solo voice. But how to give it instrumental accompaniment? Hitherto the solo voice had been submerged in the unaccompanied vocal chorus, and composers were not yet equipped with instrumental voices as plastic and consonant as those of the vocal choir, with which alone they had seriously concerned themselves. Their problem, accordingly, was to devise instrumental harmony for recitative as complete as that produced by a vocal chorus weaving polyphonic melodies. They solved it by giving the voice the support of instrumental chords, and by developing a more or less extempore accompaniment from a figured continuo. The device spread rapidly from Italy, the country of its origin. Since it placed onerous responsibility on the continuo player, it found objectors. But it was an intelligible shorthand, economized space in the score, and did not unduly tax the resources of the printer's cumbrous mechanism.

For the performance of the continuo, in Bach's time, two players at least were employed—a stringed instrument for the written notes, and a keyboard to interpret the figured chords. In chamber music a violoncello or viola da gamba partnered the cembalo. In church the weightier violone or contrabass supplemented the violoncello, and, at least in the choruses, the organ displaced the cembalo. In orchestral music the continuo was no less essential; however fully it was scored—e.g. in Bach's Brandenburg Concertos and *Ouvertures*—the cembalist and his string *confrère* were necessary to the complete interpretation of the work. Moreover, the cembalo could multiply the written sounds in different octaves; so that, by using its 4-foot and 16-foot stops, the player gave his extemporized part almost the volume of organ tone, a faculty manifestly incongruous with the principles on which modern chamber music is based. For the registers (whether controlled by stops or by pedals) enabled the player to fill out his chords extremely fully, and without additional labour on the manuals.

Professor Tovey gives an instructive illustration from the 'Trio' for Flute, Violin, and Continuo in the *Musicalisches Opfer*. Here is Bach's score:

Here is the filling out of the continuo by the cembalist in accordance with the normal practice—leaving to the violoncello the throbbing quavers:

And here is the manner in which the modern pianoforte would attempt to produce the same effect:

45

It follows from the definition of chamber music already given, and from the circumstances of Bach's career, that his *salon* music was composed mainly in the service of princely patrons. At Weimar, however, his office required him to provide cantatas for the ducal chapel, and his own inclination drew him to concentrate on the organ. Consequently, by far the larger quantity of his chamber music was composed at Cöthen. But he was not entirely neglectful of this form at Leipzig, and for a practical reason. Definite evidence is lacking, but it is probable that some of his Concertos and *Ouvertures* were written, or adapted, for two organizations not subordinate to his Cantorship. For several years he conducted one of the two musical societies (Collegium Musicum) supported by the students of the local University, a connexion which provided him with instrumentalists for the performance of his official music. Moreover, his Collegium Musicum voiced the homage of the general community when, as was not infrequent, it was honoured by visits of the sovereign or members of his family. It functioned also on occasions of lesser ceremony, as when a Professor was honoured by his students. The Society held weekly practices, and though its public concerts are neither recorded nor probable, it entertained its supporters and distinguished visitors. Bach's Cembalo Concertos would be appropriate to such occasions, and a desire to exhibit the talents of his gifted sons, in a company to which their circumstances admitted them, may have further inclined him to contribute to the Society's programmes. Another platform for his chamber music may have been provided by the royal Capelle at Dresden. He received the titular office of Court Composer in 1736 and held it till his death. He was in close touch with the personnel of that body, and it would be strange if his music were not occasionally performed by it, even if his office laid no obligation upon him to compose.

Bach's chamber music, as revealed in Table III, is cast in the *Sonatas* Italian forms his generation preferred—the Sonata and Concerto. In modern usage the former term is almost restricted to the pianoforte, and the composition is stereotyped

46

in form. Bach interpreted it simply as instrumental music contrasted with the Cantata. Nor had it yet assumed the classical three-movement design. Ten of his Sonatas are planned in Suite form (*Sonata da camera*)—three of those for Solo Violin, the six for Violoncello Solo, and the Violin-Cembalo Suite in A major. The Flute Sonata in C major is a hybrid: its three normal Sonata movements conclude with two Minuets. The others are generally arranged on a four-movement plan (*Sonata da chiesa*), in which slow *Adagios* or *Largos* alternate with quick *Allegros*, their parts, in general, being combinations of independent melodic lines, and their *Allegros*, especially, contrapuntal in design. Bach treats only the violin, flute, viola da gamba, and violoncello in this form, and the violin preponderantly, whether as a solo instrument, or above a figured continuo, or associated with the cembalo in a strict trio. Herein he reflected the taste of his period, which preferred the Sonata for a single violin to the Sonata for two, which was the distinctive type of chamber music in the seventeenth century. Prolific as he was in every form, his Sonatas exhibit no inclination to prolong Corelli's earlier style. There are extant eighteen Sonatas for a single instrument associated with a keyboard accompaniment, but only one for two violins and continuo. Nor does Bach show liking for combinations of two different instruments. He wrote only two Sonatas for Flute-Violin-Cembalo, and one for two Flutes and Cembalo in G major, probably an earlier form of the Gamba-Cembalo-Sonata in the same key.

Bach's chamber Sonatas, including Suites or Partitas, can be distinguished in four categories: (*a*) twelve for a solo instrument without keyboard accompaniment; (*b*) five for a single instrument and figured continuo; (*c*) four for two instruments and continuo; and (*d*) thirteen for a single instrument—flute, violin, or gamba—and cembalo, one of which (the Cembalo-Gamba Sonata in G) is extant in a probably earlier form for two flutes and cembalo.

The twelve Solo Sonatas in the first category demand the highest technique for their execution, and were evidently composed for exceptionally competent members of Prince

Leopold's Cöthen Capelle. The six for Violin Solo perhaps were written for Joseph Spiess, the principal violinist, who, like Bach, accompanied the Prince on his ceremonial journeys. Three of the six are in Suite form (Partita); the others are in Bach's alternate *Adagio-Allegro* style. It has already been observed that the last of them (the Partita in E major) is also claimed for the lute, and the Sonata in A minor is extant also as the Clavier Sonata in D minor. The six for Violoncello Solo perhaps were composed for Christian Bernhard Linigke, or possibly for Christian Ferdinand Abel, a viola da gamba player, whose son in later years was the partner of Johann Christian Bach in London. They are all in Suite form, and the sixth is for a five-string instrument. It is observable that Bach wrote no music for the violoncello in collaboration with the keyboard. Nor, apparently, did he write much for a wind instrument. The fragment of a Sonata in F major for Oboe, Violin, and Continuo is extant, and a Solo Sonata in A minor for Flute is published in Peters' Edition (No. 3332) from a manuscript belonging to the Rust family, of Leipzig. It is of little interest and bears no evident signs of Bach's authorship. If it cannot be summarily dismissed as spurious, the composition does nothing to strengthen the dubious authority of the manuscript.

The second category is sparsely represented in Bach's chamber music. For a solo instrument and continuo he wrote five Sonatas—three for the flute, two for the violin, and a Fugue for the latter instrument. The first Minuet of the Flute Sonata in C is exceptional for the fact that the continuo is fully set out in from two to three parts, and, generally, the Sonatas in this category are duets, having the solo instrument and the harmonized bass as their two voices. Of the two Violin Sonatas, the one in G major, apart from its inherent beauty, is interesting as having the same continuo as that of the Sonata for Flute, Violin, and Continuo in the same key. Not improbably the bass is Italian, perhaps by Albinoni, one of whose themes Bach used elsewhere. The other, in E minor, is not in pure Sonata form. It includes an *Allemande* and a *Gigue*.

In the category of two instruments and continuo only four Sonatas are extant. Two of them are for flute-violin-continuo, one of which Bach inserted in the *Musicalisches Opfer*, where it is definitely distinguished as 'Trio', and the other is constructed on the same bass as that of the Violin Sonata in G major mentioned in the preceding paragraph. A third is for two flutes and cembalo. A Sonata in C major for two violins and continuo and a Canon in C minor for Flute-Violin-Continuo (also in *Musicalisches Opfer*) are the remaining examples of Bach's art in this form. They can all be regarded as strict trios, of which the two instruments and harmonized bass are the three voices. A violoncello sounding the bass melodic line elevated it to equality with the other real parts.

Of Sonatas for a single instrument and cembalo *concertante* thirteen examples are extant. In this category Bach was not concerned to give a solo voice the support of instrumental chords, but associates the cembalo with another instrument in a contrapuntal trio, whose melodic lines are those of the participating instrument and the upper and lower parts of the cembalo. But he was not pedantically consistent in maintaining this form without variation. Passages are found, though seldom, in which the lower cembalo part is figured, while the upper part is silent. Cases of this occur in the Cembalo-Violin-Sonatas in B minor, A major, G major, F minor, and the Cembalo-Gamba-Sonatas in D major and G minor. In these instances Bach temporarily abandons an exact three-part texture, apparently to emphasize the statement of a particular theme, and for that period the trio becomes a duet between the first voice and the harmonized continuo, while the third member of the trio—the upper part of the cembalo—is silent.

Of heavier texture than the Sonatas are a number of instrumental compositions distinguished by Bach as 'Concertos'. The origins of the Concerto form *Concertos* are vocal, and are found in the sixteenth-century *concerti da chiesa* or *concerti ecclesiastici*, motets with organ accompaniment, as opposed to the traditional *a cappella* style. Its original significance persisted in Bach's usage, with whom 'Concerto' and 'Cantata' are synonymous terms, e.g. cantata No. 21 (*Ich hatte viel Bekümmernis*), whose parts are inscribed by him 'Concerto a 13'. Indeed, as Professor Tovey observes, the barriers between vocal and instrumental forms in the earlier half of the eighteenth century are so slight that Bach, 'the most accurate exemplar of all forms, is the master who achieved the most astonishing translations from one medium to the other, transcribing concerto movements into great choruses, and, conversely, turning arias into slow movements of concertos.'

Bach's instrumental Concertos number twenty-four, of which four are duplicates:

1. { The Cembalo Concerto in D major
   { The Violin Concerto in E major

2. { The Cembalo Concerto in G minor
   { The Violin Concerto in A minor

3. { The Cembalo Concerto in F major
   { The Violin Concerto in G major[1]

4. { The Concerto for 2 *Cembali* in C minor
   { The Concerto for 2 Violins in D minor

Another (for four *cembali*), in A minor, is an arrangement of Vivaldi's Concerto for four Violins, in B minor. The number of original Concertos, accordingly, is nineteen. In regard to the duplicated Concertos, it is significant that in every case the Cembalo version stands a tone below that for the violin. Whence we conclude that the Cembalo Concertos were not composed in the same period as those for the violin, but for an instrumental body whose normal chamber pitch (Cammerton) was a tone above that in use where the other set was composed. The latter were certainly written at Cöthen. Hence, their transcription for the cembalo must have been made at Leipzig, and for a purpose already indicated.

Apart from the Brandenburg set, which needs particular notice, Bach's Concertos employ only a string *ensemble*. The

[1] The 4th Brandenburg Concerto.

single exception is the Cembalo Concerto in F major, in which flutes are added. The incomplete Violin Concerto (Sinfonia) in D major, which is scored for trumpets, drums, and oboes, besides strings, is not properly chamber music, but probably served as the introduction to a lost church cantata. For his solo instruments Bach employs the cembalo (preponderantly) and violin. He wrote only one Triple Concerto, in A minor, for Cembalo, Flute, and Violin. Excepting the first and third Brandenburg, all his Concertos are in three movements: (1) a quick introductory *Allegro* or *Vivace*; (2) a slow *Adagio, Andante, Largo, Larghetto*, or *Siciliana*; and (3) a brisk *Allegro* or *Presto*, which is marked 'Fuga' in the Concerto for two *Cembali* in C major, and 'Alla-breve' in the Triple Concerto in A minor.

Bach's treatment of the continuo in the Concertos for one or more *cembali* is not quite clear. Of the seven for a single cembalo the Concerto in A major is the only one of which the original parts are extant and complete. They include, besides one for the violone, another fully figured and inscribed 'Continuo', a fact which indicates that in this instance, at least, a second cembalo supplied the harmony. Rust regarded this as proof that the other Concertos were similarly provided. But that Bach was not bound slavishly to convention is evident in the Triple Concerto in A minor, which lacks a specifically-named continuo part, but has one for 'Violoncello e Violone'; while the solo cembalo part is treated in the manner and with the significance already noticed in certain Sonatas: its bass is figured, but only in passages in which its upper part is silent. In other words, the same keyboard functions as solo and continuo. Moreover, in the middle movement—a four-part arrangement of the middle movement of the Organ Sonata for two manuals and pedal in D minor (B.G. XV, p. 32)—the three concerted instruments alone take part. Of the Concertos for two, three, and four *cembali* not a single figured continuo part exists. The addition of another cembalo to the solo instruments would be cumbrous and inconvenient, and there is no evidence that Bach employed one. On the contrary, in the middle movement of the C major

51

Concerto for two *cembali* Bach gives the direction 'Quartetto tacet', which clearly includes the violoncello (i.e. the continuo) along with the two violins and viola of the *ensemble*. In the C major Concerto for three *cembali* the bass of *all three* concerted instruments is figured in the middle *Adagio*, while the violoncello is strengthened by 'Bassi'. In brief, as Mr. F. T. Arnold, the principal authority on the continuo system, remarks, we are probably too inclined to standardize Bach's methods, and should rather conclude that, in Caesar's phrase, it was his habit 'pro re nata consilium capere' (to act according to circumstances).

Upon a larger scale and more adventurous planning than *Branden-* those composed for the Cöthen Capelle are six Con- *burg* certos known as the 'Brandenburg', since they were *Concertos* dedicated and presented to Christian Ludwig, Markgraf of that State. In his dedicatory letter, dated from Cöthen on 24 March 1721, Bach describes them as 'Concerts accommodés à plusieurs Instruments', and, on the score, as 'Six Concerts avec plusieurs Instruments'. Each, in fact, employs a different combination, and all display the three-movement form, common to others already reviewed, except the first and third. In the former Bach placates popular taste by permitting dance measures to follow the normal *Allegro*, and in the latter only two *Adagio* chords separate the opening and concluding *Allegros*.

Up to this point Bach had written pure instrumental movements for less than a dozen church cantatas, but none of symphonic proportions or requiring more than a chamber orchestra of strings and light woodwind for their performance. The opportunity to fill a larger canvas attracted him, and the Brandenburg Concertos are his earliest essays in absolute instrumental music on the grand scale. They are a remarkable expression of his fertile and adventurous mind; the wind instruments, particularly, are treated, in Schweitzer's words, 'with the audacity of genius'. We search vainly in contemporary literature for such exacting demands on their technique or such masterly success in weaving them into a polyphonic scheme.

52

Concerto No. I employs a wind *ensemble* of horns, oboes, and bassoon, supplementing the normal strings, to which a 'Violone grosso' is added, with harpsichord accompaniment (Basso continuo). There is no *concertino* of solo instruments, but the violino piccolo is prominent, and the instruments divide into three natural groups—horns, woodwind, and strings. In No. 2 a flute, oboe, trumpet, and violin form the *concertino*, with an *ensemble* of strings over the 'Violoncello e Cembalo all'unisono'. No. 3 exhibits a peculiar texture. It is scored for three violins, three violas, and three violoncellos over the 'Violone e Cembalo'. As in No. 1, the instruments are in three groups. No. 4 is in the manner of No. 2; one violin and two flutes form the *concertino*, with the strings as *tutti*. In No. 5 the flute, violin, and cembalo are concerted, with the usual string *tutti*. Excepting five bars in No. 2, this is the only Concerto of which the cembalo part is figured, and on the plan more than once observed already— the under stave is figured only when the upper one is silent. No. 6, like No. 3, is an experiment in string tone. It is scored for two violas, two *viole da gamba* and violoncello, over a continuo for violone and cembalo. Bàch's combinations exhibit remarkable variety and original orchestral contrast. They rouse enthusiasm by their rotund polyphony, splendid vigour, and glorious melody.

Four Suites or *Ouvertures*, in the style of Lully's operatic overtures, complete the tale of Bach's instrumental *Ouver-* chamber music. It is not possible to determine *tures* positively whether they were written at Cöthen or Leipzig. The two in C major and B minor, scored for strings and woodwind, were suited to the equipment of the Cöthen Capelle. The favourite one in D major, and the fourth, in the same key, are scored for trumpets and drums, oboes, bassoon, and strings, and may have been composed for Bach's Leipzig Collegium Musicum, or for the Dresden Capelle. The figured basses of the ones in C major and B minor are extant; those of the pair in D major are lost. But their form is common to all. They open with a long introductory movement, in which a brilliant *Allegro* is preceded by a stately *Largo*.

Thereafter they follow the Suite or Partita form, differing from those for the keyboard only in the displacement of the Allemande, Courante, and Sarabande by freer dance forms. No Allemande appears in the four *Ouvertures*, and a Courante and Sarabande occur only once. A Bourrée is common to them all, and a Gavotte and Minuet are in all but one. The Cöthen pair is distinguished from the other two by Bach's generous inclusion of dance measures, and an atmosphere of stately charm is common to all their old-world movements. They conjure the picture of a vanished society; indeed, in Schweitzer's words, are 'the ideal musical picture of the rococo period' in which Bach passed his life.

NOTE

THE most illuminating exposition of Bach's chamber music is Professor Tovey's article 'Chamber Music' in *Cobbett's Cyclopedic Survey of Chamber Music* (1929). See also Professor Dent's article there and the article on 'Bach'; Schweitzer, i, chap. 17; Spitta, Bk. IV, chap. 3 and *passim*; Parry, *passim*. The Brandenburg Concertos are analysed by Mr. Fuller-Maitland in the 'Musical Pilgrim' series. The classic treatise on the continuo system is Mr. F. T. Arnold's *The Art of Accompaniment from a Thorough-Bass* (Oxford University Press 1931).

V. THE 'MUSICAL OFFERING' AND 'THE ART OF FUGUE'

REFLECTING on his career in the sightless hours of his last illness, the date '7 May 1747' stood out with agreeable prominence in Bach's calendar. It was the day on which Frederick of Prussia, not yet styled 'the Great', received him at Potsdam. As a Saxon subject, Bach had little cause to regard that potentate with amity. But Frederick was already the most powerful, as he was the most observed, of German princes, a patron of music, performer of some ability, and the employer of Bach's second son, Carl Philipp Emanuel. On every count the invitation to Potsdam was welcome and flattering, and, after the event, called for respectful commemoration.

The qualities that most excited Frederick's curiosity in Bach were his notorious gift of extemporization and semi-miraculous ingenuity in contriving and developing fugal themes. To test these abilities the king invited him to treat a subject of his own royal invention, and played it to him with his own royal finger. With increasing astonishment, as Bach exhibited his powers, Frederick capped his demands with a request to hear his theme developed fugally in six parts. On a keyboard without auxiliary pedals this was an excessive test, and Bach declined it, remarking, says Forkel, that not every theme, however excellent in itself, was adapted to such treatment. He therefore substituted one of his own invention, and, 'to the astonishment of all who were present, developed it with the skill and distinction he had shown already in treating the king's theme' in fewer parts.

Of all the forms Bach's genius employed, the Fugue was the one in which he was most congenially fluent, endowing it, too, with melodic qualities hitherto not associated with it. In that sphere his contemporaries, otherwise insensitive, owned his abnormal talent, and he was himself conscious of an exclusive sovereignty in it. The natural inclination to assert it was

55

spurred by his Potsdam visit and the applause of so distinguished an audience. Moreover, his failure to satisfy
Frederick's last exacting test *ex tempore* urged him to use the
king's theme for a convincing demonstration of his powers.
On his return to Leipzig he addressed himself to the task, and,
exactly three months later, dispatched to the king the earlier
of the two supreme examples of his genius in Fugue form,
both of them closely related in time, community of principle,
and true musical eloquence—the *Musical Offering* (*Musicalisches Opfer*) and *The Art of Fugue* (*Die Kunst der Fuge*).

The *Musical Offering*, sent to the king in July 1747, pre-
Musical sented a flattering tribute to Frederick, and an
Offering elaborate memento of the Potsdam visit. At considerable cost Bach had bound in leather with gold tooling a
number of pieces in which the king's theme

was the subject of varied treatment. Engraved on five leaves,
they were prefaced by the inscription: 'Musical Offering to
H.M. the King in Prussia', a correct definition of Frederick's
sovereignty, along with a dedicatory letter of exaggerated
compliment to the king's 'right royal theme', and regret for
inadequate treatment of it at Potsdam. The apology did not
directly excuse the six-part extemporization. For this first
instalment of the *Musical Offering* contained only (1) a Fugue
(Ricercar) in three parts; (2) a 'canon perpetuus' in three;
(3) five 'canones diversi' in two and three; and (4) a 'Fuga
canonica' in three. To the last six pieces (Nos. 3 and 4) Bach
added a sub-title in his own script, a clever acrostic on the
word 'Ricercar', which associated what followed with the
occasion the composition recalled: *Regis Iussu Cantio Et Reli-
qua Canonica Arte Resoluta* (The king's theme *et cetera* treated
in canon form). Moreover, to emphasize the association, he
inscribed the fourth of the 'canones diversi' with the aspira-
tion, 'As the notes, so may the king's welfare increase!' and

over the fifth (a perpetual canon ascending a whole tone at every repetition) wrote the wish, 'May the king's glory soar with the ascending modulation!'.

Frederick, perhaps, was gratified by Bach's masterly use of his theme. But the composer could not regard his task as complete until he presented it in the six-part fugal form Frederick had particularly desired to hear. For what urgent reason he dispatched his 'Offering' before this crowning illustration of his skill was ready is not clear. Subsequently he completed it, engraved it in open score to exhibit its design, and, with two more canons, sent it to Berlin to join the earlier instalment. Some indication of the king's appreciation may have been conveyed to him; an agate snuff-box among his effects at the time of his death perhaps was a tangible expression of it. For he was emboldened to add a final instalment to his 'Offering', and in a form particularly appropriate to its recipient: it comprised a Trio in C minor for Flute, Violin, and Continuo, and a perpetual canon for the same instruments, both built upon the 'thema regium'.

The ingenuity and imagination which the *Musical Offering* displays make it, in Spitta's words, 'a monument of strict writing which will endure for all time'. Yet it lacks the artistic completeness, the systematic design, of the later *Art of Fugue*. The three-part Ricercar is a masterpiece of animated fugal writing, and its fellow in six parts is the richest illustration of Bach's genius in this *genre*. But, associated with them are exercises in canon form which stand upon another platform, and also a not wholly relevant instrumental Trio. Moreover, various in design, the pieces lack homogeneity in the voices that interpret them. The fugues in three and six parts are keyboard music, and so are most of the canons. But '2 Violini in unisono' are expressly prescribed in one of them, the Trio and concluding canon require a flute and violin, and the 'Fuga canonica' demands one or other of those instruments for the upper part. Bach, in fact, was deflected from a symmetrical design by consideration for the exalted audience he was addressing. Had the victor of Mollwitz not been the most distinguished flute-player in Europe, the *Musical Offering* would have been planned on stricter lines.

The *Musical Offering* has been aptly called 'the ante-*Art of* chamber to the *Art of Fugue*'. For the Potsdam visit *Fugue* kindled Bach's inclination to expound by example the technics of a science of which he knew himself to be the completest master. The mechanical, quasi-mathematical ingenuities of counterpoint had always interested one to whom the invention or solution of complicated canons was an agreeable relaxation. These dispositions were stimulated by his labour on the *Musical Offering*. For his canonic variations on the melody 'Vom Himmel hoch' were published at this time, and, in the few months of life that remained to him, he prepared for the engraver the series of demonstrations posthumously published as *The Art of Fugue*.

Whether Bach himself chose the title of this, his last, work is not known. Nor did he, as in the *Musical Offering*, indicate in a Preface the circumstances of its composition or the purposes it was designed to serve. But its contents leave no doubt on the latter point: they were planned to demonstrate the whole art of Fugue and Counterpoint, in its simplest and most complicated forms, including some Bach himself nowhere else employs. For this purpose, as in the *Musical Offering*, he used a motto-theme:

The theme, in itself, is not interesting, though his treatment of it makes it so. It bears obvious resemblance to the 'thema regium' of the earlier work, than which it is more concise, and with the pliability the other lacked. Indeed, the conjecture may be hazarded that it is the actual theme Bach used at Potsdam for his six-part extemporization, and that, while he rejected the subject proposed by Frederick, his own complimented the king as its ultimate originator.

The major portion of *The Art of Fugue* must have been written in 1749, when Bach already was assailed by the malady that killed him. Eleven numbers were sent to the engraver before his death, and, after it, Counterpoints XII and XIII, as well as two of the four canons subsequently included in the original published edition, were found in his autograph manuscript. Detached from it, other studies were also discovered, whose inclusion, presumably, was intended; in particular, an unfinished 'Fuga a 3 Soggetti', the concluding movement of the original published edition.

Had the work not been in large measure already engraved, it probably would have remained in manuscript, unheeded and unknown; for the filial piety of Bach's sons was not excessive. But, after a depressing attempt to attract public notice, it was published under Carl Philipp Emanuel Bach's supervision in 1752, in an edition containing fourteen counterpoints or fugues (one of which is duplicated), and four canons, all constructed on the motto-theme. The counterpoints are printed in open score, as in the case of the six-part fugue in the *Musical Offering*, and all are in four parts except No. VIII (in three) and No. XIII (in three). The last movement is incomplete, and of a final counterpoint, with which Bach intended to conclude the work, no trace was discovered among his papers. To balance these omissions the editor inserted the supremely beautiful, but irrelevant, Choral Prelude on the melody 'Vor deinen Thron tret ich hiemit'. The reception of the work was distressingly apathetic. So few copies were purchased, that Carl Philipp Emanuel sold the plates for the price of the metal and communicated his indignation to Forkel, who angrily scolded his compatriots for their disregard of a masterpiece, a castigation not entirely deserved; for the treatise was offered to a generation which no longer recognized the Fugue as the architrave of the musical structure.

In *The Art of Fugue* all possible fugal types are represented in movements which Sir Hubert Parry justly calls 'astounding examples of Bach's dexterity'. 'We do not know which to wonder at most,' comments Schweitzer, '—that all these combinations could be devised by one mind, or that, in spite of the ingenuity of it all, the parts always flow along as naturally and freely as if the way were not prescribed for them by this or

that purely technical necessity.' Wonder is especially excited by
Counterpoint XIII. Here we have two three-part fugues, each
the exact and complete inversion of the other, their three
parts being so contrived that the middle one of the upper
becomes the treble of the lower, its treble becomes the bass,
and its bass the middle. For seventy-one bars Bach carries on
this stupendous and orderly complication, each part in each
bar being an exact inversion of the other, as though it were
reflected in a mirror:

Counterpoint XII is in the same mirror-form. And here
the two related fugues are in four parts, the treble, alto,
tenor, and bass of the one being inverted to form respectively the bass, tenor, alto, and treble of the other. Its long
sustained notes are not suited to the keyboard. Hence Bach
did not arrange it for two harpsichords as he did No. XIII.

The last Counterpoint, in Bach's manuscript and in the
original edition, ends abruptly at bar 239, where a note by Carl
Philipp Emanuel states that the composer's death left it unfinished. To that point the movement is built upon three new
themes, the third of which spells BACH in the German notation:

Since the motto-theme common to all the preceding movements does not make its appearance in the completed 239 bars, Rust, who edited the work for the Bachgesellschaft in 1878, concluded that the fugue was erroneously introduced into the original edition and formed no part of Bach's design. Spitta, too, supposed that it 'crept in by misunderstanding', and Schweitzer expressed the same opinion. They are in error. Martin Gustav Nottebohm (d. 1882) pointed out that the motto-theme can be combined with the three new subjects of the unfinished fugue, and Professor Tovey, working independently, has actually completed the fugue by introducing it, an achievement of scholarship which vindicates the work's earliest editor. Moreover, the same pen has completed Bach's scheme by constituting a final fugue in accordance with authoritative indications of the principles on which the composer planned to build it.

The work is therefore before us, we may suppose, in accordance with its author's design, a stupendous exposition of its title, 'but not within the range of practical music', Sir Hubert Parry declares. Here, too, Professor Tovey has delivered Bach from his commentators. For in *The Art of Fugue*, he shows, Bach has written keyboard music as genuine and accessible as that of *The Well-tempered Clavier*.

NOTE

THE text of the *Musical Offering* is printed in Peters' edition (No. 219). That of *The Art of Fugue*, edited by Professor Tovey, is published by the Oxford University Press, along with his *A Companion to the Art of Fugue* (1931) and separate numbers arranged for the piano. The text in open score, with a valuable preface by Wilhelm Rust, was published in the Bachgesellschaft edition in 1878, and, in a supplementary volume edited (1926) by Wilhelm Graeser, whose orchestral transcription of the work is very impressive. An elaborate analysis of *Die Kunst der Fuge* by Erich Schwebsch is published (1931) by the Orient-Occident-Verlag (Stuttgart). See also the *Bach-Jahrbuch* for 1924 and 1926. For the two works dealt with in this section see generally Spitta, vol. iii, chap. 5; Schweitzer, vol. i, chap. 18; and Parry, chap. 15.

VOCAL

VI. THE CHURCH CANTATAS AND ORATORIOS

OF all the forms in which he expressed himself, Bach was most prolific in the Cantata; for in no other was the call upon him so continuous and persistent. His Cöthen chamber music records merely an episode in his productivity. His organ music was not written under the compulsion of duty, and his other keyboard music was no less voluntary in its inspiration. But the composition of church cantatas was an obligation which rested on him, with the briefest intermissions, throughout his professional career. His earliest can be dated 1704, his latest 1744, and in that interval of thirty years nearly three hundred came from his fecund pen. Their *libretti* stirred his imagination in varying degree. But this surprising record of official duty shows no sign of flagging, of perfunctory approach, of jaded effort. It declares, rather, the unplumbable resources of his genius; for no limits to his inventiveness appear. Till the very end the well of his inspiration yielded its waters with generous spontaneity, and melodies of the most fragrant beauty flowed at his easy command. Only a sense of the sacred dignity of his task can have sustained him on this high level of accomplishment. For even if convention headed his cantata scores with the petition 'Jesu, help me!' and ended them with the ascription 'To God alone be the praise', those words in his masculine script truly reveal the spirit in which, throughout his life, he approached the most continuous and onerous duty of his professional career.

The Church Cantata, known to us almost exclusively in *Church* Bach's inspired examples, was the particular product *Cantatas* of his period and hardly survived him. After his death it was generally ejected from the church service; the historical establishments, vocal and instrumental, maintained for its performance decayed; and other forms of musical expression superseded it. In some degree it corresponds

62

with the Anglican Church Anthem. Both constitute an act of praise which excludes the general congregation, save as a silent auditor. On the other hand, the Church Cantata was usually, and in Bach's case invariably, performed with an orchestral accompaniment in which the organ, though active, was seldom an obbligato performer. Consequently the Cantata was on a larger scale than the Anthem: those composed by Bach were planned to last for about thirty minutes, a welcome break in a lengthy service.

The Cantata differed from the Anthem also in the fact that it was admitted to only one of the several diets of Lutheran public worship, a service distinguished as 'Hauptgottesdienst', the principal one on Sundays and holy days. The cantata had its place in it as the 'Hauptmusik' (principal music), or, simply as 'die Musik' (the 'Music'); for music of elaborate type was not otherwise normally admitted to it. Different towns had their peculiar uses: for instance, cantatas were sung during Advent at Weimar, but not at Leipzig. Universally, however, in towns provided with the necessary equipment, the cantata was sung at 'Hauptgottesdienst' on Sundays and other appointed feasts or days of civic observance. At Leipzig fifty-nine annual occasions were thus distinguished, and it was the Cantor's principal duty to provide for them a cantata, either from his own pen, or from the choir's library, or from some other source accessible to him. Like other persons holding a similar office, this duty compelled Bach to copy the scores of other composers, a fact which has caused music to be attributed to him of which he was not the author. Thus, during his Leipzig Cantorate he was responsible for the provision of a cantata, from one source or another, on about sixteen hundred occasions. Towards that formidable total we know, on good evidence, that he contributed five complete annual cycles of his own composition, two hundred and ninety-five cantatas in all. About thirty were in his portfolio when he went to Leipzig. So, between 1723 and 1744 he composed two hundred and sixty-five, an average of one cantata each month, a calculation confirmed by the conditions of his service at Weimar, which prescribed a similar monthly quota. About two-thirds of these compositions survive, a proportion which can be accounted large, in view of the indifference towards all but his organ music manifested by the generations that followed him. In the Bachgesellschaft edition they fill nineteen volumes and part of another, a monument of duty which only the inspiration of high purpose can have prevented from becoming irksome.

The service which admitted the cantata was co-ordinated with a particular purpose—to bring into prominence the Gospel for the Day. For, whereas the Anglican Protestants framed a new Order of Morning Prayer, Luther prescribed a service which followed the Roman Mass in outline and, to some extent, in detail. It began with the 'Kyrie' and 'Gloria in excelsis', sung by the choir, a portion of the service significantly distinguished as the 'Missa' or Mass. Then the Epistle was read, and, after a congregational hymn suited to the season had been sung, the Gospel was ceremoniously intoned in Latin at the altar. Then followed the 'Credo' (Creed), also recited in Latin, and an interval of solemn relaxation was reached. The Belief had been affirmed, the Gospel had been intoned, and would again be read from the pulpit in the vernacular. At this point therefore music was invited to assist the exposition of the Gospel topic. Here, accordingly, the cantata was performed to a libretto as closely based on the Gospel text as the Sermon which followed it. Occasionally the cantata was in two Parts, in which case the second followed the Sermon and preceded the Administration of the Holy Communion, which, about noon, brought to an end a service continuous since seven in the morning. Thus, Bach's cantatas are not intelligible unless we realize that, when writing them, he placed himself in the pulpit, as it were, to expound the Gospel in the language of his art. To the task he brought a mind versed in theological dialectic, and a devout spirit resolved to clothe his exposition in the most persuasive form of which his art was capable.

Historically, as its name declares, the cantata was Italian, a development of the *cantata da chiesa*, whose distinctive features—declamatory recitatives, solo arias, and orchestral interludes—are referred to Giacomo Carissimi, who died only eleven years before Bach's birth. From Italy the cantata passed to Germany, where it established itself as the 'Hauptmusik' of the principal morning service. The earlier German cantatas, however, those of Albert, Schütz, and Hammerschmidt, exhibit the simpler structure of the original *cantata da chiesa*, and have little affinity with Bach's massive compositions. For he brought to their composition the elaborate technique acquired on the organ. Nor was the admission of the cantata to the church liturgy universally approved, since it associated divine worship with the apparatus of Opera. Conservative tradition preferred a more austere model, and in his earliest cantatas Bach conformed with it. They contain no recitatives, and the arias are of the German Arioso type. But, supported by the ablest critic of that generation, the innovators prevailed, and, in the early years of the eighteenth century, Erdmann Neumeister, a young deacon at Weissenfels, evolved a type of libretto which Bach thereafter consistently adopted, since it gave the fullest scope for musical expression in the recitative and aria forms. In general, it consisted of six or seven numbers relative to the Gospel for the day—rhymed stanzas suited to treatment as a chorus or aria, others in poetic prose for solo recitative, occasionally a Bible verse, and generally, to conclude, the stanza of a congregational hymn. Bach used several of Neumeister's texts, and other writers who supplied him at Weimar and Leipzig conformed to that model. Towards the end of his career Bach liked to treat the complete text of a congregational hymn in this manner, using its first stanza for his opening chorus in an elaborate treatment of the hymn's melody, and its last for his closing Choral, paraphrasing its intermediate stanzas for the intervening arias and recitatives. These 'Choral Cantatas' are the finest examples of his genius in cantata form, and, to congregations familiar from childhood with the hymns and melodies he used, must have been deeply impressive. But in construction they differ not at all from those based on a free libretto. In both types the first movement is generally a chorus and the last a Choral, in which the congregation almost certainly took part, the intervening movements being treated as arias and recitatives for solo voices. Sometimes, but seldom, the choir's participation in the cantata is confined to the closing Choral, and the preceding movements are allotted to a solo voice or voices. But Solo Cantatas are infrequent and merely indicate the temporary inability of Bach's choristers to take their normal part.

Naturally, the cantata was performed only in communities able to maintain the expensive apparatus its performance demanded. The singers were provided by the Town-schools (Stadtschulen), such as St. Thomas's at Leipzig, of which Bach was Cantor (choirmaster). The orchestra was a mixed body of amateurs and professionals, the latter of whom, at Leipzig, numbered eight, on whom Bach chiefly relied for his trumpet, horn, oboe, and timpani parts. For his strings he was largely dependent on undergraduates (*studiosi*) of the local university and foundationers (*alumni*) of St. Thomas's School. His ordinary orchestra consisted of strings, flutes, and oboes, and he rarely used instruments already obsolescent—the lute, viola da gamba, and viola d'amore. For festival occasions he added to his score trumpets and drums, restricting them generally to the opening chorus and concluding Choral. But on no occasion were his performers numerous. His players might number ten or twelve and the singers seventeen, for only his *coro primo* was sufficiently expert to perform cantata music. Nor was the cantata heard in all the Leipzig churches, but only in the two principal ones, St. Thomas's and St. Nicholas's, in whose organ galleries on their western walls singers and players assembled for this purpose on alternate Sundays under Bach's direction.

Nowhere else in his music do we so closely approach the mind of Bach as in his cantatas; for they reveal the deeps of his character, the high purpose to which he dedicated his genius. Already as a schoolboy he was serious beyond his years, and throughout his life religion was his staff and comfort. With what vivid literalness he read his Bible is evident in the music with which he clothed its text. And of the

Lutheran hymn-book his exposition is so intimate that, even in his Choral Preludes, which lack words, we can not seldom detect in his music the stanza that was in his thoughts and guided his pen. Thus, the music of the cantatas is a faithful mirror in which the mind of their composer is revealed. They disclose the fact that his astonishing fecundity was controlled by searching and frequent pondering of the texts he set. They reveal the keenness and clarity with which he visualized Bible scenes and characters. How consistent and devotional, for instance, is his portrayal of the Saviour's gracious dignity! And, after hearing the several Michaelmas cantatas, who can doubt that Bach pictured Satan, not as Isaiah's Lucifer, the Day Star, the Son of the Morning, but as the malignant and cumbrous Serpent of *Genesis*, the Great Dragon of *Revelation*? For always Bach depicts his rolling gait in writhing themes, which outline his motion as clearly as an etcher's pen. With what tender touches he paints the scene of the Nativity! And with what poignant emotion he follows the Saviour's footsteps to Calvary! With truth, therefore, Schweitzer observes that the cantatas are the most reliable indicators of Bach's genius and character. For their range is so wide, they reflect him from so many angles, and express him in so many moods, that they reveal his personality no less than his art.

It is a comedy of contradiction that a man emotional in every fibre should have been, almost until our own generation, regarded as a cold mathematical precisian. The portrait is a travesty, and its persistence due, in no small measure, to ignorance of Bach's musical language. In his cantatas it can be studied over a wide field of observation, and (as has already been remarked[1]) may be described as one of realistic symbolism, expressing particular moods and signifying particular actions by melodic, or rhythmic, figures. And the idioms never vary. For Bach's language, developed to its fullest in the cantatas, is employed in almost the earliest of his compositions, especially in the *Orgelbüchlein* planned at Weimar. It is, indeed, the most consistent musical idiom known to us, and also the most precise. For though his

[1] See p. 21 *supra*.

mature experience devised shadings and inflexions, the root symbols are constant in his usage and dissipate at a breath the false notion of him as a cold formalist.

Within the restricted compass of these pages it is only *Chorals* possible to lay out a general plan of this spacious territory over which Bach's genius presides. There is, however, one feature common to all the cantatas that calls for notice. In the apparatus of Lutheran public worship the Hymn-book, next to the Bible, was held in peculiar affection and regard. Bach's love for the Chorals, i.e. the Lutheran hymns and their melodies, was profound; his intimate acquaintance with them is evident in his wide and appropriate use of them. For they were in the very blood of his people, an essential adjunct of their devotional equipment.

On its admission to the service of religion, therefore, it was inevitable that the cantata should add the Choral to its otherwise secular and foreign ingredients. From Bach's cantatas Chorals are rarely absent, their original cruder settings replaced by his gorgeous harmonies. His treatment of their melodies, so familiar and so beloved, is one of the most beautiful features of the cantatas, and the wealth of ingenuity he expended upon them reveals the deep regard in which he held them. He was not satisfied to introduce them only in their simple four-part hymn form, though that type of Choral is the most frequent in his scores. Often, and in his 'Choral Cantatas' invariably, he treats the melody (set always to its original stanza) in an elaborate chorus with his fullest contrapuntal skill, after the fashion of the organ Choral Preludes. Again, he gives us what are conveniently distinguished as 'Extended Chorals', simple four-part settings, but with each line of the melody separated from its neighbours by interludes, usually, but not invariably, instrumental. Then, we have the 'Unison Choral', in which one or more voices sing the hymn melody above a free instrumental accompaniment. Less frequent are Chorals which Bach styles 'Aria', in which the melody is woven into the texture of the movement by various devices, sometimes as a solo, more frequently as a duet, and once as a trio. More curious,

68

and less satisfying, is the 'Dialogue Choral', fashioned as a conversation between two voices, to one of which are allotted the words and melody of the hymn, while the other carries on a free commentary. Bach marks these movements 'Recitative' or 'Recitative and Choral', and if they are more curious than agreeable, they declare his intention to display the Choral in every form it was capable of assuming. Beyond all these in number, and in the affection they command, are the simple, hymn-like, four-part Chorals which decorate his cantatas like jewels of price. Even his own generation, otherwise indifferent towards his vocal music, regarded them as masterpieces. They are marvels of melodic part-writing, the utterance of a mind deeply moved by words hallowed by tradition and usage.

The following Table concisely relates Bach's cantatas to the occasions for which they were composed. They *The* are indicated by the numbers allotted to them in the *Cantatas* Bachgesellschaft edition, those of the pre-Leipzig *seasonal* period being distinguished by italic type. It will be *order* noticed that the cycle of five cantatas, which Bach is said to have composed, is complete for only five of the occasions for which cantatas were required—Christmas Day, New Year's Day (Feast of the Circumcision), Purification of the Virgin Mary, Easter Day, and the Inauguration of the Civic Council. It will be observed also that the celebration of the three High Festivals was continued on the two succeeding days, and that on both of them cantatas were performed at Leipzig.

69

THE CANTATAS IN SEASONAL ORDER

Advent I. 36, *61*, 62.

„ II. *70*.

„ III. *141*. See also *186*.

„ IV. *132*. See also *147*.

Christmas Day. 63, 91, 110, *142*, 191, Christmas Oratorio, Pt. I, 'Ehre sei Gott' (incomplete).

„ Second Day. 40, 57, 121, Christmas Oratorio, Pt. II.

„ Third Day. 64, 133, 151, Christmas Oratorio, Pt. III.

Sunday after Christmas. 28, 122, *152*.

Circumcision (New Year's Day). 16, 41, 143, 171, 190 (incomplete), Christmas Oratorio, Pt. IV.

Sunday after the Circumcision. 58, 153, Christmas Oratorio, Pt. V.

Epiphany. 65, 123, Christmas Oratorio, Pt. VI.

Epiphany I. 32, 124, 154.

„ II. 3, 13, *155*.

„ III. 72, 73, 111, 156.

„ IV. 14, 81.

Purification B.V.M. 82, 83, 125, 157, *158*. See also *161*.

Septuagesima. 84, 92, 144.

Sexagesima. *18*, 126, 181.

Quinquagesima (Esto mihi). 22, 23, 127, 159.

Annunciation B.V.M. 1. See also *182*.

Palm Sunday. *182*.

Easter Day. 4, *15*, *31*, *160*, Easter Oratorio.

„ Monday. 6, 66.

„ Tuesday. 134, 145. See also *158*.

Easter I. (Quasimodogeniti). 42, 67.

„ II. (Misericordias Domini). 85, 104, 112.

„ III. (Jubilate). 12, 103, 146.

„ IV. (Cantate). 108, 166.

„ V. (Rogate). 86, 87.

Ascension Day. 11 (Oratorio), 37, 43, 128.

Sunday after Ascension Day (Exaudi). 44, 183.

Whit-Sunday. 34, *59*, 74, *172*.

„ Monday. 68, 173, 174.

„ Tuesday. 175, 184.

Trinity Sunday. 129, 165, 176, 194.

Trinity I. 20, 39, 75.

Trinity II. 2, 76.
St. John. 7, 30, 167.
Trinity III. *21*, 135.
   ,,   IV. 24, 177, *185*.
   ,,   V. 88, 93.
   ,,   VI. 9, 170.
Visitation B.V.M. 10, *147*, *189*.
Trinity VII. 107, 186, 187.
   ,,   VIII. 45, 136, 178.
   ,,   IX. 94, 105, 168.
   ,,   X. 46, 101, 102.
   ,,   XI. 113, 179, '*Mein Herze schwimmt im Blut*' (*c.* 1714).
   ,,   XII. 35, 69, 137.
   ,,   XIII. 33, 77, 164.
   ,,   XIV. 17, 25, 78.
   ,,   XV. 51, 99, 100, 138.
   ,,   XVI. 8, 27, 95, *161*.
   ,, XVII. *47*, 114, 148.
  ,, XVIII. 96, 169.
St. Michael. 19, 50, 130, 149.
Trinity XIX. 5, 48, 56.
   ,,   XX. 49, *162*, 180.
   ,,   XXI. 38, 98, 109, 188.
   ,, XXII. 55, 89, 115.
   ,, XXIII. 52, 139, *163*.
   ,, XXIV. 26, 60.
   ,,   XXV. 90, 116.
   ,, XXVI. 70.
  ,, XXVII. 140.
Inauguration of the Civic Council (*c.* August 30). 29, *71*, 119,
    120, 193.
Reformation Festival (October 31). 79, 80, 192? See also 76.
Wedding. 195, *196*, 197, Three Wedding Chorals. 'O ewiges
    Feuer' (incomplete). 'Herr Gott, Beherrscher' (incomplete).
Mourning. 53, *106*, 118, *131*?, *150*?.
Occasion not specified. 54, 97, 117.

To eight cantatas—the six Parts of the *Christmas Oratorio*,
the *Easter Oratorio*, and the *Ascension Oratorio*— *Oratorios*
Bach gives the title 'Oratorium'. They are not
conspicuous by their design, but they share a characteristic

which caused Bach to distinguish them by this name from his other cantatas—they dramatize the incidents of the three festivals which commemorate the Saviour's mortal career. With lyrical commentary the *Christmas Oratorio* unfolds the Gospel narrative in six 'Parts', one of which served as the cantata on Christmas Day, others on the two following days, the Feast of the Circumcision, the Sunday after the Circumcision, and the Feast of the Epiphany. In the *Easter Oratorio* the actual Bible text is not used. But the episode of the empty sepulchre is dramatically told, and the solo parts are allotted to Mary Magdalene, Mary the mother of James, and the Apostles Peter and John. The *Ascension Oratorio*—printed as cantata No. 11 in the Bachgesellschaft edition—repeats the *Christmas Oratorio* design: the circumstances of the Ascension are narrated in St. Luke's words and those of the *Acts*.

Bach's genius was Teutonic in its inclination to complete a design. The *Christmas Oratorio* was performed between Christmas Day 1734 and Epiphany 1735. The other two must be attributed to the latter year and its successor (1736). The reasons which moved Bach at this particular time to adopt the title 'Oratorio' and to exhibit the characteristics of that form are obscure. Probably he was influenced by the example of Dresden, where the vogue of the Oratorio was popular at that period.

NOTE

DETAILED analyses of the cantatas are afforded by Spitta, Schweitzer, and Parry. A general guide to them is provided by the present writer in 'The Musical Pilgrim' series. The cantata *libretti* and their relation to the Lutheran liturgy can be studied in his *'Bach's Cantata* Texts' (Constable, 1926). For Bach's use of the orchestra in them, see his *Bach's Orchestra* (Oxford University Press, 1932), and, for the Chorals, his *Bach's Chorals*, Part II (Cambridge University Press, 1917), and *Bach's Four-part Chorals* (Oxford University Press, 1929).

VII. THE PASSION MUSIC

FROM pre-Reformation times it was the Good Friday custom at Leipzig to rehearse the Passion story in the narrative of one of the Evangelists—simple plainsong recitative, with short four-part chorus-settings of such portions of the text as invited that form of utterance. The continuity of this simple musical idiom was not broken until 1721, two years before Bach's appointment to the Cantorship, when, for the first time, the story of the Passion—'Vom Leiden und Sterben Jesu Christi'—was sung in St. Thomas's to concerted music in the new style. Bach's setting of St. John's text was next heard in that church in 1723, and, thereafter, St. Thomas's and St. Nicholas's were alternately the scene of similar annual performances.

Throughout Bach's Cantorship the Passion music was performed at Good Friday Vespers, a service held *Passion* at a quarter to two in the afternoon. It began with *Music* the ancient Passion-tide hymn, 'When Jesus on the Cross was bound' (*Da Jesus an dem Kreuze stund*). Part I of the Passion music followed, and, after it, a hymn and the sermon. Part II of the Passion music was then sung, followed by the four-part motet 'Ecce quomodo moritur justus'. The Good Friday Collect was next intoned, Martin Rinkart's hymn 'Now thank we all our God' was sung, and the lengthy service concluded with the Blessing. Such was the liturgical setting of all Bach's *Passions*.

The earliest catalogue of Bach's compositions, published four years after his death, enumerates 'Five Passions, one of which is for double-chorus'. The number tallies conveniently with the five annual cycles of church cantatas attributed to him on the same authority. It is, however, neither probable, nor is there convincing evidence, that he wrote so many *Passions*. Some of the movements of a setting of St. Mark's narrative survive in another context, and it is not unlikely that he put music to a *Passion* libretto published by Picander, his Leipzig librettist, in 1725. But the *St. Luke Passion*, attributed to him in the Bachgesellschaft edition in 1898, bears no trace of his authorship. Thus, he certainly composed three, perhaps four, but not five *Passions*. There was, indeed, no need for a larger number; for, though twenty-seven Good Fridays fell within his Cantorship, there is reason to believe that his own *Passions* were sung exclusively in St. Thomas's, and, if so, were required on only thirteen occasions. So few opportunities hardly called for five separate settings. The evidence of its parts suggests that the *St. John Passion* received at least three performances. The *St. Matthew Passion*, produced in 1729, was almost certainly repeated in 1736, on the third anniversary of its original performance. In other words, two Good Fridays (1731 and 1734: no performance was given in 1733) passed at St. Thomas's between the two dates. For the first Bach wrote the *St. Mark Passion*. The second may have witnessed the third performance of the *St. John*. At least it is clear that by 1731 Bach had composed such a number of *Passions* as, heard in rotation, could not become stale by repetition or require augmentation.

The earliest of Bach's *Passions*, that according to St. John, *St. John* was composed during the winter of 1722–3, and was *Passion* performed in St. Thomas's on 26 March 1723, a month before his formal appointment to the Leipzig Cantorship. It was written at Cöthen in circumstances of indecision and difficulty, while the success of his candidature hung in the balance. Hence, his choice of St. John's text was probably deliberate. It is by far the shortest of the four Gospel narratives, omits many incidents of the Passion story, and therefore sets the composer a lighter task than, for instance, St. Matthew's chapters, from which, however, Bach borrowed the incidents of the Earthquake and Peter's remorse. Thus the narrative portion of the *Passion* consists of chapters xviii and xix of St. John's Gospel, along with three verses from St. Matthew's. To these Bach added fourteen simple four-part Chorals of his own selection, and twelve lyrical stanzas for the first and last choruses and aria and arioso movements. Nine of them he borrowed from the phenomenally popular *Passion* libretto written some ten years earlier by Barthold Heinrich Brockes, of Hamburg, a text which Bach, almost alone among contemporary composers, did not put to music in its entirety. Its length probably deterred him, and his conservative prejudices must have abhorred its rhymed version of the Bible text. Nor did he accept Brockes's lyrics without subjecting them to critical and improving revision.

Not yet in touch with those who aided him later at Leipzig, and long since removed from his Weimar literary collaborators, Bach appears either to have constructed the libretto himself, or to have called in a helper as little expert. For it bears evident proofs of unskilful construction. The two Parts are unequally balanced, and the distribution of lyrical movements is awkwardly contrived, a blemish for which the Bible text is in large measure responsible. Bach was aware of these deficiencies, and for subsequent performances deleted five movements, two of which he transferred to other scores. The more notable of the two is the supremely masterly Choral chorus 'O Mensch, bewein'' (O man, bewail thy grievous fall!), which formed the opening movement of the *St. John Passion* in 1723, but was subsequently transferred by Bach to its present position in the *St. Matthew Passion*.

The *St. John Passion* is on a smaller scale than its greater successor, less devotional, and therefore less moving. But its action is swifter, and its atmosphere more tense and dramatic. Their contrasted qualities are due to the differing character of the Passion narrative in the two Gospels. St. Matthew's is rich in episodes which invite lyrical commentary or pious meditation. St. John's is poor in situations which admit them. Beginning abruptly with Judas's treachery, it is in the main the narrative of the Saviour's trial before the High Priest and Pilate. The story, sustained and continuous, affords few halts for reflective repose; an air of passion, the clamour of fierce hatreds pervades it, and finds animated expression in Bach's vivid choruses, which carry the action onward to its relentless climax.

Beyond the general contrast their respective texts invited, Bach's treatment of the two Passion narratives differs in

75

details. In the *St. John Passion* the Saviour's utterances are
not haloed by an accompaniment of strings, as in the later
work. Nor does His personality display the gracious be-
nignity so characteristic of the *St. Matthew Passion*. The
earlier work, too, exhibits a characteristic almost unique in
Bach's practice—of three choruses he repeats the music
to different words, and actually employs that of another three
times. It is suggested that these repetitions were deliberate,
and that Bach intended thus to emphasize the rancorous
obstinacy of the priests and people. But it is difficult to
believe that he would have repeated himself so frequently,
and sometimes ineptly, had not his original score been written
in haste and under the pressure of circumstances. Its in-
congruity with his text accounts for his discarding the Choral
chorus 'O Mensch, bewein'', with which the work originally
opened. Not the frailty of man, but the majestic personality
and patient suffering of the Victim are the themes of the
Fourth Gospel, and at Leipzig Bach subsequently found
a librettist whose text for the substituted movement exactly
reflected the Evangelist's standpoint:

> Lord, show us in Thy Passion's smart
> That truly Thou Eternal art,
> God's Only Son,
> Who e'en affliction did'st not shun,
> Yet reign'st victorious.

For Good Friday 1725, when it was again the turn of St.
Picander's Thomas's to hear the Passion music, Bach not
Passion improbably used a libretto published by Picander
in that year. It was modelled on Brockes's text, but of shorter
length and coarser quality. The Passion story is narrated in
the barest outline, its incidents are detailed without devotional emphasis, Chorals are almost entirely excluded, and the
Saviour's voice is heard only twice, in a single aria in each
Part. Such a libretto cannot have satisfied Bach; yet, at this
early period of his Leipzig career, he may not have been un-
willing to collaborate with Picander in a *Passion* of the
popular type. His association with him in similar works in

76

1729 and 1731 lends further support to the supposition. The fact that the score is not extant is, unfortunately, no disproof that it existed.

In 1727 Bach gave a revised version of the *St. John Passion* in St. Thomas's. But in 1729 he produced there St. Matthew a new work, to which only the Mass in B Minor is Passion comparable, the deepest and most moving expression of devotional feeling in the whole of musical literature. Picander published the libretto of the *St. Matthew Passion* at Easter 1729. We do not know when he first placed it in Bach's hands. A work of such magnitude and profundity of treatment must have engaged the composer absorbingly over a long period. Portions of it were first heard at Cöthen three weeks before the production of the complete work at Leipzig. They formed the major part of the *Trauer-Music* commemorating Prince Leopold, who died in November 1728. Bach either offered or was invited to compose it. Absorbed, however, in the composition of the *Passion*, he found it inconvenient to provide an original work, and therefore belatedly invited Picander to fit new and appropriate words to nine of the completed *Passion* movements, borrowed another from another score, and performed the work with his own singers at Cöthen. The score was extant in 1802, but has surprisingly disappeared. The conjecture that Bach borrowed from it to complete the *Passion* cannot be entertained.

Having regard to the materials at his disposal, and of his outspoken opinion of their quality a few months later, it would astonish us that Bach should have planned so large a canvas at this time, were it not elsewhere evident that at no period was his genius daunted by circumstances. The libretto of the *St. Matthew Passion* is of exceptional length. Its narrative portion—chapters xxvi and xxvii of the Gospel—contains 141 as against the 82 Bible verses of St. John's text; its lyrical stanzas number twenty-seven as against the twelve of the earlier work. The score, too, is planned on a scale of unexampled magnitude. It demands two separate and independent musical bodies—two four-part choirs, each supported

77

by its own orchestra of strings, flutes, oboes, harpsichord, and organ. The solo voices are not equally distributed. All the Bible text, except one short passage, is allotted to Choir I. Hence, members of that body sang the music allotted to Jesus, the Evangelist, Peter, Judas, Pilate, the two Priests, Pilate's wife, and the two Maids. Bach entrusted to Choir II only the few bars sung by the two False Witnesses. His unequal treatment of the two choral bodies has a practical reason. Choir I was composed of his best singers, by whom his weekly cantatas were performed. Choir II was formed by his less efficient 'Motet choir', which functioned on Sundays in that one of the two principal churches in which the cantata was not sung. Thus, its participation in the *Passion* music was outside its customary experience, and the music beyond its normal capacity. For that reason Bach allotted the solo movements to the more expert body, and the few four-part choruses entrusted to Choir II are short and relatively simple.

In no other work is Bach's close study and picturing of his text so evident as in the *St. Matthew Passion*. Its opening chorus—'The Road to Calvary'—is a stupendous canvas such as Gustave Doré might have limned. Amidst a company of Roman soldiers Bach places the Man of Sorrows. The music moves with unrelenting rhythm above a throbbing pedal-point which symbolizes the weary Saviour. On either hand the faithful Zion's sons and daughters raise their voices in poignant threnody as they see pass before them the Cross and its Bearer, the sacrificial Lamb. At that word the heavens unfold and a celestial choir acclaims the Victim in the melody of the German 'Agnus Dei'. It is one of the most vivid canvases in Bach's gallery. To each Choir, too, he gives a peculiar individuality. In the first Part the two exclusively represent the Believers; in the second Part they generally voice the hatred of the Saviour's enemies. In both impersonations Bach distinguishes them. Choir I speaks for the Twelve, the core of the Christian community: Choir II, for the wider body of believers. Excepting a few movements which express a more universal emotion, the two bodies do not coalesce, a

device by which Bach indicates the numerical insignificance
of the Christian band. As the voice of the fanatic Jews, Bach
is at equal pains to regulate the utterance of the two Choirs.
Usually they are heard together as discordant bodies in a universal clamour. Sometimes, but rarely, they unite in unison,
intent upon a common purpose, as in the shouts 'Let Him be
crucified!' and 'His blood be on us!' They are heard in
unison in their derisory calls to the Saviour to descend from
the Cross. But later, when the idle crowds have departed and
the watchers are few, Bach places them in two groups about
the Cross. To Choir I he gives the words, 'He calleth for
Elias', to Choir II the half-expectant cry 'Let be, let us see
whether Elias will come and save Him'. But he unites
them in the awed admission, 'Truly this was the Son of
God'.

The closer we study the *St. Matthew Passion* the more
evidently is it the work of a mind intimately familiar with and
profoundly moved by the Gospel text. The short chorus 'Not
upon the feast', the first of the incisive choruses which distinguish the later from the earlier *Passion*, puts an accent of
alarm upon the words which they do not seem to support.
Clearly, Bach collated St. Luke's text (xxii. 2) and read there
'for they *feared* the people'. Again, St. Matthew and St.
Mark both record the Saviour's words, 'Eli, Eli, lama
sabachthani', as the last He spoke, the expiring cry of His
anguished humanity. For the only time, therefore, Bach
withdraws the halo which hitherto had irradiated His every
utterance. The accompanying strings are silent, and the
organ takes their place. A final illustration: Only St.
Matthew puts the words 'Truly this was the Son of God' into
the mouth of the centurion *and others*. Bach accordingly
unites his Choirs in this act of reluctant homage. Of such
a pondering and devout mind the *St. Matthew Passion* is the
creation. It is one of our civilization's incomparable masterpieces, and at the most solemn season of the Church's year
unites Protestant Christendom in pious emotion; for, in
Parry's concise appreciation, it is 'the richest and noblest
example of devotional music in existence'.

St. Thomas's Church provided a perfect platform for Bach's music. It is as large as a small cathedral, a late Gothic, three-aisled fabric without transepts, and with a narrow chancel set out of line with the nave. It has an air volume of some 640,000 cubic feet, and in Bach's time its walls were dotted with 'swallows' nests' or private boxes. To-day it accommodates a congregation of 1,800 persons, and its reverberation figure is about half that of an English Gothic church of the same size, but about one second in excess of that of a similarly sized concert-hall. Thus the building represents a compromise between a church and a secular concert-room, and has other acoustic advantages. The source of sound is well placed; for the level vault directs the tone from the choir and orchestra and organ in the west gallery down to the congregation without creating marked 'echo paths'. In Bach's time this advantage was the greater because his forces were placed somewhat higher than at present. Other advantages were the large resonant wood area, the unicellular nave, and absence of transepts. Moreover, the church has no 'note' of fixed tonality, and no special region of response. Thus it is not tied to the reciting note or 'Collect tone' usual in large buildings.

The Reformation intimately affected church acoustics: it admitted vernacular German to a place beside ecclesiastical Latin in the Liturgy; and it altered the internal structure of church buildings. The congregation no longer assembled to adore a Mystery, but to listen to the homily of a preacher elevated and visible. Hence, to the already existing western gallery, which housed the organ, were added side galleries and gallery boxes, a change which altered the reverberation, and therefore the acoustic quality of the edifice as a musical auditorium. The congregation was enlarged in proportion to the air volume, and reverberation—the time taken for a sound to die away after the source has ceased—was correspondingly shortened. This favoured the use of the vernacular; for, whereas the broad open vowels and delicate consonant divisions of medieval Latin are best heard in a Gothic church whose reverberation is long, the vivid

St. Thomas's

80

German consonants have a greater audibility and less reverberation.

In brief, Bach's platform was ideal for the production of his music. It was equally sympathetic to the vowel tones of German and Latin (and in Latin much of the Liturgy continued to be rendered). Its moderate reverberation permitted the performance of organ music with a rapid bass, which, in other conditions, becomes a confused roaring. The absence of a 'reciting note' released Bach from considerations of tonality. No strain was imposed on his immature soloists. Voices and orchestra were complementary, and while the tone of the strings benefited from the large wood area, the outline and design of the music was easily and instantly perceived.

The Good Friday of 1731, when it again fell to St. Thomas's to hear the Passion music, found Bach in no mood *St. Mark* to provide such a work as he had produced in 1729. *Passion* His relations with the civic Council were not cordial, for he had seen cause recently to offer acrid comment on the materials with which he was expected to make music. His domestic amenities, also, were seriously disarranged by the Council's resolution to reconstruct the Schoolhouse in which he had his lodgings. For the Good Friday music of 1731 he therefore commissioned Picander to give him a libretto which should make no heavy call upon him, and Picander complied with one based upon St. Mark's narrative. Modelled upon the *St. Matthew Passion*, it employed the literal Bible text (chapters xiv and xv), and punctuated it with a liberal provision of Chorals and a limited number of original lyrical stanzas. To five of the latter Bach fitted music from the *Trauer-Ode* of 1727, and to the other three almost certainly adapted old material. The Bible text also conveniently relieved him from the need for considerable effort. For St. Mark's chapters are remarkable for the paucity of passages suited for settings as choruses. There are only ten, and assuming that Bach treated them on the same scale as in the *St. Matthew Passion*, which contains them all, he needed to write less than one hundred bars of music. The *St. Mark*

Passion, in fact, was a piece of deft carpentry, so faintly remembered that the score was offered for sale in 1764 as the work of an unknown composer! It is no longer extant.

It is not surprising that Bach should have shrunk from re-experiencing the stress and emotion which had brought the *St. Matthew Passion* to birth, a work so intimate in its utterance that, as M. Pirro has remarked, it seems to be embroidered with tears and tinged with flames and blood. Not again could Bach ascend those heights or explore those *St. Luke* sacred deeps. In fact, after 1731, he did not again *Passion* re-write the Passion tragedy. But in one of the immediately following years he probably performed a *Passion* based on St. Luke's Gospel, which is unhappily included among his genuine works in the Bachgesellschaft edition. Less than half the score is in his autograph, and the music itself yields not a trace of his inspiration. Either it was the immature work of one of his sons, or one of the many works by other composers which his office compelled him to copy for his choir's usage.

Apart from the unsurpassable glory of the music with which *Operatic* he endowed it, it is Bach's distinction to have rescued *Passion* Passion music from degrading associations which threatened to divorce it completely from the service of religion. Early in the eighteenth century it succumbed to the popular inclination to dramatize the Bible text in a libretto which substituted rhymed stanzas for the Bible verses, ejected Chorals, and applied to the sacred drama the apparatus of the Opera. The flippant irreverence of these dramatic *Passions* had already stirred a reaction before Bach turned his genius to this form. But it was his individual achievement to have purged it of its impurities, infused a devotional intention into the operatic forms—aria and recitative—it employed, and restored the Choral to its fitting place as the vehicle of congregational devotion. He triumphed as much by the noble elevation of his purpose as by the impressiveness of his genius. The operatic *Passion* vanished from North Germany during his lifetime, surviving elsewhere only where the influence of Italian Opera prevailed. Since his death the

Passion has been treated by composers either in cantata or oratorio form. None has ventured to trespass upon a domain over which his sovereignty is unchallenged.

NOTE

ANALYSES of the *Passions* are in Spitta, vol. ii, chap. 7; Schweitzer, vol. ii, chaps. 26, 28; Parry, chaps. 5, 6. See also the present writer's two volumes on the *Passions* in 'The Musical Pilgrim'. Miniature full scores of both works are published by the Eulenburg and Vienna Philharmonischer Verlag. The autograph score of the *St. Matthew Passion* is reproduced in facsimile by the Insel Verlag, Leipzig.

VIII. THE FUNERAL MUSIC

A FEW of Bach's cantatas, notably the 'Actus tragicus' (No. 106, *God's time is the best*), are of funerary character, *Cantatas* and for two occasions of public mourning he composed cantata music on a larger scale—the *Trauer-Ode* for the Queen-Electress of Poland-Saxony in 1727, and the *Trauer-Music* for Prince Leopold of Anhalt-Cöthen in 1729. At ordinary commemorations of deceased persons, however, Leipzig custom prescribed that the music should be in the severer motet style, without organ or orchestral accompaniment, in a service thus ordered: 1. Hymn; 2. Sermon; 3. Motet; 4. Collect; 5. Blessing.

To attend the funerals of departed citizens was a public *Funerals* obligation the scholars of St. Thomas's, Leipzig, shared with other town-schools throughout Germany. Rich and poor alike received this formal valediction. But the number of scholars who attended varied according to the status of the deceased and the ability of his survivors to pay the regulated fee. The Cantor's attendance was similarly conditioned, and his fixed, but not considerable, income was materially augmented by receipts from this source. Preceded by the cross-bearer, the school processed to the house of mourning and thence to the churchyard outside the city walls, singing hymns and other music of simple character. If the deceased was well-to-do, or prominent in the community, the service of commemoration, already outlined, would be held on a subsequent Sunday afternoon, when, for the motet, the Cantor would usually draw upon the choir's repertory. Occasionally he composed music specially for the occasion, either at the request of the mourning relatives, or in accordance with the deceased person's will, in which it was not unusual to bequeath the customary fee of one thaler for the purpose, and even to prescribe the text of the commemoration sermon.

84

Bach does not appear to have often received the 'Motet thaler'. Only six motets by him are extant, one of *Motets* which doubtfully bears a funerary character:

1. *Singet dem Herrn ein neues Lied.*
   (Sing to the Lord a new-made song!)

2. *Der Geist hilft unsrer Schwachheit auf.*
   (The Spirit helpeth our infirmities.)

3. *Komm, Jesu, komm.*
   (Come, Jesu, come!)

4. *Fürchte dich nicht.*
   (Be not afraid!)

5. *Lobet den Herrn, alle Heiden.*
   (O praise the Lord, all ye nations!)

6. *Jesu, meine Freude.*
   (Jesu, Joy and Treasure.)

Only one of the six can be positively associated with a particular occasion. According to Bach's autograph, *Der Geist hilft unsrer Schwachheit auf* was composed for the burial of Johann Heinrich Ernesti, Rector of St. Thomas's School, who died on 16 October 1729. Alone of the six, Bach provided it with orchestral accompaniment, which indicates its repetition at a commemorative service in the University, of which Ernesti was Professor of Poetry; for the University was not subject to the veto on organ and orchestra which regu lated the civic churches. With less certainty, two of the remaining motets can be attached to occasions of similar solemnity. For Frau Käse, the wife of Leipzig's chief postmaster, who died in 1723, a service of commemoration was held on the Eighth Sunday after Trinity (18 July). The sermon was preached from Romans viii. 11, and as the text of *Jesu, meine Freude* is taken from that chapter, it is extremely probable that Bach's motet was composed for the occasion. On 4 February 1726 Frau Winkler, wife of the Captain of the Leipzig civic guard, was commemorated in similar circumstances. The text of the sermon was Isaiah xliii. 1 and 5, part of the libretto of Bach's *Fürchte dich nicht*. The same

85

inference may be legitimately drawn as in the case of *Jesu, meine Freude*. We lack similar clues in regard to the other three motets. But the text of *Komm, Jesu, komm* clearly declares its funerary purpose, and, despite its jubilant opening and closing sections, the words of the middle movement of *Singet dem Herrn* leave no doubt as to the ceremony for which it was composed. Of *Lobet den Herrn* it is impossible to speak with assurance; its qualities distinguish it from the others and raise doubts as to its funerary purpose.

Though written for similar uses, Bach's funerary motets are not uniform in design or structure. Four of them—Nos. 1, 2, 3, and 4—are in eight parts for two choirs. *Jesu, meine Freude* is set for five voices (S.S.A.T.B.); *Lobet den Herrn*, for four. But, excepting the last, they all display the characteristics of the German funeral motet—into their fabric, though in different ways, are woven the words and melody of a congregational hymn. In the middle movement of *Singet dem Herrn* Coro II sings the third stanza of Johann Graumann's hymn 'Nun lob, mein' Seel', den Herren!' while Coro I inserts an independent vocal interlude between the lines of the Choral melody. In *Der Geist hilft* and *Komm, Jesu, komm* the Choral concludes the motet in simple four-part harmony, Luther's 'Komm, heiliger Geist' being used in the first, and in the second an anonymous hymn set to one of Bach's tenderest aria-like melodies. In *Jesu, meine Freude* the Choral is treated variously in a series of movements which alternate with free choruses.

Besides the authentic six, two other motets, wrongly *Spurious* attributed to Bach, are familiar in English usage: *Motets* *Blessing, Glory, Wisdom, and Thanks* (*Lob, und Ehre und Weisheit*) was almost certainly composed by his early Leipzig pupil Georg Gottfried Wagner; *Ich lasse dich nicht* (*I'll not let thee go*), infelicitously translated *I wrestle and pray* in Novello's edition, is certainly the work of Bach's relative and early mentor, Johann Christoph Bach, of Eisenach. *Sei Lob und Preis mit Ehren*, No. 8 of Breitkopf's edition of the motets, is a remodelled version of the chorus 'Nun lob, mein' Seel', den Herren' of cantata No. 28, one of a few choruses in true motet style found in Bach's cantatas, their association with which puts them in a different category from those under consideration.

Bach's motets display at its highest altitude of inspiration the genius for full-throated song he inherited from his Thuringian ancestry. Their massive virility gives them pre-eminence among their kind, and, alone of his vocal compositions, they were not shadowed by the eclipse that obscured him and his art in the century that followed his death. For their performance they demand the highest qualities of choral technique, and, of all the music Bach wrote, afford the most unalloyed pleasure to the singer.

NOTE

FOR the motets see Spitta, vol. ii, chap. 9; Schweitzer, vol. ii, chap. 31; Parry, chap. 7; and the volume on the *Magnificat*, Masses, and Motets by the present writer in 'The Musical Pilgrim'.

IX. THE LATIN MUSIC

BACH'S Latin music includes a *Magnificat*, the 'High Mass' in B minor, four miscalled 'short' Masses, and five settings of the *Sanctus*. They were all composed at Leipzig, and their Latin texts were in keeping with its liturgy, which had continuously employed the language of medieval Christendom for these parts of public worship. It is noteworthy that the Masses and *Sanctus* correspond in number with the cycles of cantatas and *Passions* attributed to Bach in the earliest (1754) inventory of his music.

Lutheran practice followed the ancient Church in treating *Magnifi-* the *Magnificat* as an evening canticle, a song of *cat* praise, the counterpart of the *Te Deum* in the Morning Office. It was an old custom at Leipzig to sing it in Latin at Vespers on the three high festivals of Christmas, Easter, and Whitsun. More recently its elaborate performance with orchestral accompaniment was customary, and a setting of it for Christmas Day was the first work on a large scale undertaken by Bach after his appointment to the Cantorship. Between the movements of the Christmas *Magnificat* it was customary to insert appropriate Christmas music, apparently to accompany some kind of Mystery play enacted in the church. For the interpolated movements illustrated the incidents of the Nativity as the Gospel unfolds them: first, the angels' announcement to the shepherds, then the scene at Bethlehem, next the angelic anthem (*Gloria in excelsis Deo*), and, finally, the homage to the Holy Babe. In its first state (in E flat) Bach's *Magnificat* included these movements. He omitted them from his revision of it for the Easter and Whitsun festivals, and put it into his festival key of D major, in which it is now invariably sung.

The Latin *Magnificat* is distinguished from Bach's larger choral works by its conciseness. Scored for full orchestra—trumpets, drums, wood-wind, and strings—it contains less than 600 bars, and so is considerably shorter than the 'Credo' of the Mass in B minor. This compactness was imposed by

88

the conditions under which the work was performed. As part of a service which began about 1.45 p.m., it followed the sermon, which, with announcements from the pulpit, exceeded one hour's duration. Moreover, as has been already observed, its performance was lengthened by interpolated pieces. Conciseness was imperative in order that the service might conclude before daylight faded on a December afternoon.

In the *Magnificat*, as in the Mass in B minor, Bach declares himself no narrow Protestant. In its Latin text he read the adoration of the Church Universal across the centuries. The sustained polyphony to which he sets the first and last clauses of the canticle, the emphasis he gives to the words 'omnes generationes' (all generations), and his employment of five-part vocal harmony, all indicate an intention to make his music the voice of homage timeless and universal. In the lay-out of his score he exactly observes the divisions of the Bible text, with the significant exception of the 'omnes generationes', which he detaches for particular treatment. Otherwise, each stanza of St. Luke's text is set as a separate section, in movements equally divided between concise choruses and arias for solo voices lacking the *da capo*. As in the Mass in B minor, Bach brings the work to an end on a broad Catholic plane. For the chorus 'Sicut locutus est' is a five-part fugue on an austere theme, in the objective style of the older masters of polyphony, from which Bach passes to the dazzling brilliance of the 'Gloria'. His sense of form required him to give his work constructive unity by linking its first and last movements, as in the Parts of the *Christmas Oratorio*. The concluding 'Sicut erat in principio' (As it was in the beginning), accordingly, is a jubilant repetition of the theme of the opening 'Magnificat'.

In accordance with traditional use, the *Sanctus* was sung at Leipzig in the ancient language as part of the Communion office in the principal morning service *Sanctus* (*Hauptgottesdienst*). Its use, however, was restricted to festal seasons. For ferial occasions the prescribed order was as follows:

1. The Lord's Prayer, intoned by the minister at the altar.

2. The Prayer of Consecration.

3. The Distribution.

At festal seasons the Lord's Prayer was displaced by a Proper Preface, intoned at the altar by the minister, followed by the *Sanctus*, sung by the choir in the gallery. Simple plainsong settings of the angelic anthem were used in Bach's period of office, and also one in simple six-part harmony, a fact of interest in relation to his six-part setting of the words in the High Mass in B minor. Bach's five examples are more elaborate, and in every case have orchestral accompaniment. Probably they were heard only at the high festivals, at which, it would appear, the B minor *Sanctus* also was performed; for a separate score and parts of it in Bach's autograph are extant. Of the five shorter settings, one of the two in D major is for a double choir: the rest are for four-part chorus. Only the one in C major is scored for drums and trumpets, a fact which indicates its performance on a high festival, probably on Christmas Day 1723; for it is in the key of the cantata (No. 63) which had already been sung before the sermon.

Unlike other Protestant Churches, which substituted *The Missa* another form of morning worship for the Roman Mass, the German Lutherans continued to use the Communion Office as the principal service (*Hauptgottesdienst*) on Sundays and festivals. Nor did they reject the word 'Mass' (*Missa: Messe*) to describe it. The Leipzig Prayer-book of 1694, authoritative in Bach's lifetime, styles the service 'The Office of the Holy Mass or Communion', and those parts of the ancient liturgy which Luther retained— the *Kyrie*, *Gloria in excelsis*, *Credo*, and *Sanctus*—continued to be recited in the ancient language of the Roman ritual. But, in the usage of Bach and his contemporaries, the word 'Missa' (Mass) had also a particular and restricted meaning. It denoted the *Kyrie* and *Gloria in excelsis* together, as distinct from the *Credo* and *Sanctus*. There is no evidence that Bach ever used the word in its Roman sense. His autograph score of the Mass in B minor is in four separate sections, each with its own title-page. The first section, which contains the *Kyrie* and *Gloria*, alone bears the indication 'Missa'. There is no general title-page, and the designation 'High Mass', by which the work is generally known, was not given it by Bach, but by his son. It is, in fact, a Lutheran 'Missa', with additions which make it also a complete Roman Mass; while the other four Masses Bach composed, containing only the *Kyrie* and *Gloria*, are complete Lutheran Masses and therefore miscalled 'short'.

Thus, in that they were of practical utility, the four Lutheran Masses may have been prepared by Bach for the Leipzig churches, though their length would inconveniently prolong a service otherwise almost intolerably long. They were written subsequently to his application for the post of Court Composer at Dresden, but are not suited to the Roman ritual. If there is any connexion between the period of their composition and his appointment, they may have been offered as marks of his skill and testimonies of loyalty, for which purpose he had presented the *Kyrie* and *Gloria* of the B minor Mass in 1733. But the four differ from the latter in an important particular. Though Bach subsequently used old material to complete it, the B minor in its first state was almost completely an original composition. The four are adaptations of music originally written to other texts and for other occasions. Of the twenty-four sections into which they are divided, all but five are positively identified with movements in ten cantatas composed by Bach between the years 1723 and 1737. Consequently they are rarely performed. For, though the process of adaptation was generally accomplished with extraordinary labour and skill, and the transformation is often complete, it is preferable to hear the music in its original context.

Bach sent the *Kyrie* and *Gloria* in B minor to Dresden in 1733, with a request for the post of Composer to the Electoral Court. He received it in 1736, and there- *Mass in B minor* after completed the score by adding the other movements proper to the Roman Mass. But the dimensions of the completed work entirely forbid the supposition that he contemplated its ritual performance in church. Nor, in fact, does he appear to have sent to Dresden the additional movements the Roman liturgy required. Moreover, though he cannot have been ignorant of the Roman text, he was at no pains to follow it. In the duet (No. 7) 'Domine Deus' of the *Gloria* he writes 'Jesu Christe *altissime*' (Jesu Christ most High), though the word 'altissime' is not canonical, and would not have been admitted to the chapel of a Roman Catholic sovereign. Apparently Bach was made aware of the fact; for the word is omitted in the four other settings of the *Gloria*. The *Sanctus*, too, yields an instance of Bach's divergence from the canon. As sung at Leipzig its text accorded with Roman usage—'pleni sunt coeli et terra gloria tua' (Heaven and earth are full of *thy* glory). Bach substitutes 'eius' (his) for 'tua' (thy), and so converts an act of ritual worship into a devotional statement. More noteworthy is his general treatment of the *Sanctus*. According to Roman use, the *Osanna* and *Benedictus* form with it a single text, heralding the impending advent of the Saviour in the accomplished Mystery. Bach treats the *Sanctus* by itself, and places the *Osanna* and *Benedictus* apart in a separate section—the fourth and last— of his completed score. Therein he followed Leipzig custom, intending the *Sanctus* to stand alone, isolated in the tremendous grandeur with which his music endowed it. In it, as Professor Tovey remarks, 'Bach is himself beating time to the angels swinging their censers before the Throne.' Finally, he neglects to treat the *Agnus Dei* as a threefold petition; it should conclude twice with the prayer 'miserere nobis', and, for the third time, with 'dona nobis pacem'.

The question therefore arises—What purpose impelled Bach to complete a work as unsuited to the Roman as to the Lutheran ritual? There are three reasons, which, in fact, are complementary. In the first place, from our earliest introduction to him, Bach confronts us as a student irrevocably urged to explore the types and principles of his art. Inevitably, therefore, he was attracted to a form of musical expression in which, down the ages, composers had been inspired to express their noblest thoughts. He had copied and studied the Masses of the Italian masters: to express his own adoration in their manner was an obligation imposed on him by the instincts of his whole career. In the second place, his genius was architectonic. A torso was abhorrent to a mind by nature constructive and orderly. But, chiefly, he was moved by a deeper motive. As the Mass was the supreme act of Christian adoration, so in the ritual of the Mass music fulfilled its highest function. Bach's ingrained piety compelled him to offer the homage of his art in this form, and though, as has been shown, he writes habitually with a Protestant pen, the Mass as a whole is neither Roman Catholic nor Lutheran, but the expression of his individual idealism.

The absence of a practical purpose, which can be charged against the Mass as a whole, cannot be brought against its component parts. Their texts were common to the ritual of both Churches, and, though there is clear evidence that they were never heard at Dresden, their usage at Leipzig is in all cases probable, and, in some, certain. Three of the eight movements of the *Gloria* are extant in a separate score, and the rubric 'Post Orationem' (After the sermon), which separates them, indicates that they were sung as a cantata, in two Parts, divided by the sermon. The *Credo* (Creed) was usually intoned by the minister; and on feast-days Luther's version of it was sung. But it is not improbable that the B minor setting was heard on some occasion of particular solemnity; for in 1780 it was sung to Haydn's music. The existence of a separate score and parts of the *Sanctus* has already been stated; their provision certainly evidences its performance. The *Benedictus* was sung at Leipzig only when the *Sanctus* also was used. Bach's setting would therefore be of service, if not at other times, at least when the B minor *Sanctus* was performed. As to the *Agnus Dei*, an ancient Lutheran rubric prescribed its use during the Distribution of the Bread and Wine, when communicants were numerous. Thus, if the Mass as a whole was unsuited to the Lutheran ritual, there was no bar, other than their length, against the separate performance of its component movements. And their length might not appal a congregation agreeably accustomed to excessively prolonged diets of public worship.

Bach's borrowings from himself present a problem which

his circumstances to some extent resolve. Loaded with an onerous obligation to compose or provide a ceaseless routine of church music, and to transcribe the parts, the temptation to repeat himself was considerable. Since he did so, flagrantly, in the four Lutheran Masses, we may conclude, either that the call for them was urgent, which is improbable, or that his interest in them was perfunctory, which is likely. But there was no compulsion on him to complete the Mass in B minor, and therefore no urgency. It is unthinkable that he lost interest in a work voluntarily undertaken, and his character forbids us to imagine him capable of giving anything short of his best in such a labour. Yet the completed Mass is to some extent borrowed from older scores. In round numbers it contains 2,300 bars, rather less than one-third of which (638) are borrowed. Therefore, since it is impossible to believe that the fount of his inspiration ran dry, and as the process of adaptation involved labour at least as arduous as the composition of original material, we must suppose that, when he repeats himself, he does so because an earlier utterance offered itself as the best for his purpose.

The autograph score of the Mass in B minor is in four separate sections. The first contains the 'Missa' (*Kyrie* and *Gloria*); the second, the 'Symbolum Nicaenum' (Nicene Creed: *Credo*); the third, the *Sanctus*; the fourth, the *Osanna*, *Benedictus*, and *Agnus Dei*. The first (*Kyrie* and *Gloria*) includes eleven movements, two of which (in the *Gloria*) are borrowed material. The second (*Credo*) is in eight movements, three of which are adaptations. The fourth (*Osanna*, &c.) has four movements, all of which are found in other scores. Thus, the nearer Bach draws to the conclusion of his labour, the more he uses old material, as though the splendour of the *Sanctus* momentarily stunned his creative power.

Bach's age was not as sensitive as ours regarding the adaptation to sacred uses of music originally inspired by a secular theme. All but one of the borrowed movements of the Mass, however, are transferences from one church score to another. The single exception—the *Osanna*—a double

chorus planned on the largest scale, is also found in one of
Bach's secular cantatas, and it is of interest to determine
which of the two versions was the original. That the music
is completely appropriate to its sacred text is not question-
able; it is, in fact, as Professor Tovey remarks, 'better suited
to the heavenly hosts than to the poor mortals to whom Bach
was beholden!' In its secular context the chorus is the opening movement of the cantata *Preise dein' Glücke*, performed at
Leipzig on 5 October 1734 in honour, and in the presence,
of the King-Elector Augustus III of Poland-Saxony. The
king's visit coincided with the anniversary of his birthday on
October 7, for which Bach had prepared a cantata—*Schleicht,
spielende Wellen*—and performed it on the auspicious date.
But, arriving at Leipzig on October 2, the sovereign intimated
his pleasure that the anniversary of his election to the Polish
Throne on October 5 should receive recognition on that date.
A libretto was hastily written, in which the composer's task
was made easier by the profuse inclusion of declamatory
recitatives, and also by the provision of lyrics that suited
music already in his portfolio. For one of the three arias
Bach drew upon the *Christmas Oratorio*, which had not yet
been heard at Leipzig. Of the two choruses, the last is a
straightforward piece of spirited music which would give
Bach no more trouble than the labour of putting it on paper.
But the opening chorus is a stupendous creation, and, though
it would be rash to declare him incapable of completing it in
thirty-six hours, it is highly improbable that he did so.
Moreover, it is incredible that he should have instructed his
librettist to ease his task by putting new words to old music
for one, if not more, of the arias, and yet should have accepted
from him a stanza calling for original and elaborate eight-
part chorus treatment. There is, in fact, no reasonable doubt
that the *Osanna* was already on paper as part of the uncom-
pleted Mass, and that under stress of circumstances Bach
adapted it to the secular text.

Of the movements common to the Mass and other sacred
works there is no doubt that the latter present the original
form, excepting the *Benedictus*, the music of which is found,

also as an alto aria, in the *Ascension Oratorio* (cantata No. 11). The latter can only be approximately dated as 'about 1735', and therefore its priority to the Mass music can neither be affirmed nor denied. The two movements, however, are not identical. The cantata aria contains 79 bars, the *Benedictus*, 49. Moreover, more than half the former is so entirely different in material, that if, in fact, the *Benedictus* was adapted from it, the task must have been as onerous as the composition of a new aria.

Except in so far as it illuminates the ways of genius, it is not profitable to explore the proportion of original to adapted music in the Mass. Even in their conversion, the borrowed movements reveal the sensitiveness of Bach's judgement, the sureness of his touch. As it stands, the Mass is the fabric of a superb architect, perfect in proportion, unerring in balance.

NOTE

FOR Bach's Latin music see Spitta, vol. ii, chap. 5 and vol. iii, chap. 2; Schweitzer, vol. ii, chaps. 26 and 33; Parry, chaps. 5 and 8. See also the present writer's volumes on the Masses and *Magnificat* in 'The Musical Pilgrim'. The full score of the *Magnificat* is published in miniature by Eulenburg, and of the Mass in B minor by the Vienna Philharmonischer Verlag. A facsimile of the autograph score of the latter is procurable from the Insel Verlag, Leipzig. Of many sets of programme notes of the Mass in B minor, Professor Tovey's, prepared for a performance of the work at Edinburgh on 5 March 1931, is noteworthy.

X. THE SECULAR CANTATAS

AT no period was the composition of secular cantatas in the regular routine of Bach's official duty. His productivity in this form consequently was intermittent, his output small. The titles of less than forty works survive, and the scores of rather more than half are extant. So few, indeed, can be attributed to his spontaneous initiative that we must suppose him indifferent to this art-form. Excepting *Phoebus und Pan*, his Collegium Musicum at Leipzig does not appear ever to have performed any but the 'command' cantatas in honour of visiting royalties. His somewhat contemptuous attitude towards the Opera is on record. There is no trace of his association with it at Leipzig, and at Dresden he was tolerant of, rather than attracted by, its inanities. His nature was too serious, his estimate of music's function too exalted, to draw him actively to that form of it. It follows that his cantatas—the name by which he generally denoted them—were either 'command' tributes to princely personages, flourishes which custom required him to supply; compliments to public dignitaries; decorations of opulent weddings; or embellishments of public ceremonies. The number of those which do not fall into one or other of these categories is small.

Excepting Chorals, which are naturally absent from them, Bach's secular cantatas do not differ in construction *Drama* from those written for church use, and the music of *per* some is common to both. Most of them are lightly *musica* scored for strings and wood-wind, with the occasional addition of a horn—a chamber orchestra suited to a chamber platform. But Bach employs trumpets and drums in seven scores, most of which were performed in the open air by the light of torches. To these, and another, he gives the title 'Drama per musica', or simply 'Drama', i.e. Opera. *Angenehmes Wiederau*, though having the same characteristics, is styled 'Cantata'. In all of them there is either action or declamatory dialogue, and in all but two the solo voices

97

represent allegoric characters. They are all equipped with a Chorus, which invariably opens the work and brings it to an end. None of them has an Overture, and only one of them (*Vereinigte Zwietracht*) is provided with incidental instrumental music. They are Bach's nearest approach to the operatic stage, and some of them, not improbably, were presented as costumed masques. They were composed at Leipzig in the following order:

1. *Der zufriedengestellte Aeolus* (The placating of Aeolus). Performed on 3 August 1725 to celebrate the name-day of Professor August Friedrich Müller, whose students, or colleagues, commissioned Bach to compose it. The characters are Pallas, Pomona, Zephyrus, and Aeolus. Eager to release the imprisoned winds to devastate the flowers and forests, Aeolus is in turn importuned to relent by Pomona and Zephyrus, but yields to Pallas on learning that the Muses on Helicon are celebrating the distinguished Müller's name-day.

2. *Vereinigte Zwietracht* (Sweet voices harmonious). Performed in December 1726 to celebrate the appointment of Dr. Gottlieb Kortte as Professor of Roman Law in the University of Leipzig. The characters are Glück (Fortune), Dankbarkeit (Gratitude), Fleiss (Diligence), Ehre (Fame), each of whom eulogizes, or predicts high fortune for, the distinguished lawyer. Bach used the arias and choruses eight years later for *Auf, schmetternde Töne*.

3. *Phoebus und Pan*. Performed by Bach's Collegium Musicum in 1731. He wrote the work with the same intention as Wagner in *Die Meistersinger*. The characters are: Phoebus, Pan, Momus, Mercurius, Midas. In the character of Midas, the counterpart of Beckmesser, Bach trounces a recent and unfriendly critic of his art. The action is dramatic: Phoebus (Bach), challenged by Pan, engages with him in a contest of song. Midas declares Pan the victor and is punished with a pair of ass's ears and relegation to the back-woods, whose music he preferred. Produced on the stage by the British National Opera Company some years ago, the work discovered a charm of the first degree.

98

4. *Die Wahl des Herkules* (The choice of Hercules). Performed in 1733 to celebrate the birthday of the Crown-Prince of Saxony. This is the only 'Drama' in which Bach does not employ trumpets and drums. Two *corni da caccia* take their place. The characters are: Wollust (Pleasure), Tugend (Duty), Merkur (Mercury), and Hercules. In the character of Hercules the Prince is invited to follow Pleasure or Duty. He chooses Duty for his mentor, whereupon Mercury extols him as Saxony's Crown Prince, 'virtuous Friedrich'.

5. *Tönet, ihr Pauken!* (Thunder, ye drum-rolls!). Performed on 8 December 1733 in honour of the Queen-Electress Maria Josepha of Austria, consort of Augustus III. The characters are Bellona (War), Pallas (Wisdom), Irene (Peace), and Fama (Renown), who, from their several standpoints, acclaim their 'Queen of hearts', the 'Queen and Pearl of royal ladies'.

6. *Auf, schmetternde Töne!* (Peal, shattering fanfares!). Performed on 3 August 1734, the name-day of Augustus III. There are no *dramatis personae*, but each of the four solo voices extols the sovereign with conventionally fulsome flattery. The king was not present, and Bach used the opportunity to repeat the music of *Vereinigte Zwietracht*, composed in 1726.

7. *Preise dein' Glücke!* (Praise thy good fortune!). Performed on 5 October 1734, on the anniversary of Augustus III's election to the throne of Poland. Written in haste (see p. 95 *supra*), there are no *dramatis personae* and only three solo voices, each of which, in an aria and recitative, recites the virtues and prowess of the sovereign.

8. *Schleicht, spielende Wellen!* (Flow gently, fair rivers!). Performed on 7 October 1734, on the birthday and in the presence of Augustus and his queen. The characters are the four rivers, Pleisse, Donau (Danube), Elbe, Weichsel (Vistula). Vistula and Elbe, the chief rivers of Poland and Saxony, assert their particular possession of Augustus. Danube, as representing Austria, the country of the sovereign's queen, contests their claim. Pleisse decrees that Danube must resign her contention and the others share their sovereign. To this they agree, and unite in supplication for Augustus's welfare.

99

9. *Angenehmes Wiederau* (Pleasant fields of Wiederau). Performed at Wiederau on 28 September 1737 on the formal accession of Johann Christian von Hennicke to his estates. The characters are Zeit (Time), Glück (Good Fortune), the river Elster, Schicksal (Fate), each of whom offers welcome to the new lord of the soil. Excepting the recitatives, Bach used the music for church cantata No. 30 (*Freue dich, erlöste Schaar*).

It is an interesting reflection that Bach might have been *Court* required to write for the stage, had not his ducal *cantatas* master at Weimar turned from the theatre to the pulpit before Bach entered his service, and if Prince Leopold of Cöthen had not lacked the means to support a dramatic establishment. Consequently Bach's secular compositions in his pre-Leipzig period are *cantate da camera*. The earliest, *Was mir behagt*, was composed in honour of Duke Christian of Weissenfels, for performance at a banquet following a day's hunting on 23 February 1716, when the Grand Duke of Weimar and others were guests. The work is lightly scored for flutes, oboes, strings, and (befitting a hunting theme) *corni da caccia*. The characters are, Diana, Pales, Endymion, and Pan. Diana, wooed by Endymion, rejects his advances: the hard-riding Christian absorbs her thoughts on this day of his festival. Pan surrenders his sovereignty of the woodlands in which the hero displays his prowess, and Pales, god of shepherds and flocks, pays similar tribute. In conclusion the four unite in fervent aspirations for Duke Christian's happiness.

At Cöthen Bach composed the remaining examples of his work in this form. Probably in 1718 he wrote a 'Serenada' for the Prince's birthday, entitled *Durchlaucht'ster Leopold*. It is lightly scored for flutes and strings, there are no *dramatis personae*, and only two voices are employed—a soprano and a bass-baritone. The soprano music probably was sung by Bach's wife, Maria Barbara, whose tragic death occurred a few months later. The libretto is of customary banality. In 1721 or 1722 Bach composed another cantata of similar character, *Mit Gnaden bekröne*, which, like the earlier, is

45410

written for two solo voices, an alto and a tenor, but with a
concluding movement in which they are joined by a soprano
and a bass. Other Cöthen cantatas were composed in 1723
and 1726, but their music is lost, or exists in another context.
These, with the others on a larger scale already noticed,
complete the tale of Bach's court compositions. Ready as,
no doubt, he was to subscribe to the divine right of princes,
even the conventional text of his librettos could not impede
the flow of his inspiration. In fact, they invited some of his
jolliest and most exhilarating music.

Reference has been made to the 'Cantata' *Angenehmes
Wiederau.* One other stands in the same category as *'Homage'*
a 'homage' cantata. On 30 August 1742, Carl Hein- *cantatas*
rich von Dieskau, Chamberlain of the Saxon Exchequer,
received the homage of his tenants as Lord of the Manor
(Gutsherr) of Klein Zschocher and Knauthain, near Leipzig,
to which he succeeded on his mother's death. Picander held
a post under him, and wrote a libretto for the occasion, which
he entitled 'A burlesque Cantata', *Mer hahn en neue Oberkeet*
(We've got a new squire). It is generally known as the
'Peasant Cantata', for its characters are a couple of peasant
lovers, and its language, in parts, the dialect of Upper
Saxony. Bach evidently delighted in a text thoroughly
natural and abnormally negligent of the stilted demigods of
mythology. It is lightly scored, in the style of a village
orchestra, has only two singers, a soprano and bass, and is
unique in the possession of an overture (a Quodlibet), and
in Bach's quotation of folk-melodies. There is no action, but,
in short movements, many of them popular dance measures,
the young sweethearts praise the new Lord of the Manor and
his wife, deplore the exactions of the taxman and recruiting-
sergeant, are grateful to the new squire for lightening them,
and, with a final duet, retire to a drinking booth to dance and
be merry. In no other work is Bach's wig so evidently removed from his brow, in none his zest for the melodies of
the countryside so generously displayed. Only his wedding
Quodlibet, to be noticed later, matches it in this quality.

In the category of satyric operetta *Phoebus und Pan* has

been mentioned. Upon a smaller scale, and in less acid
Satyric mood, the 'Coffee Cantata' *Schweigt stille, plaudert
operettas nicht* must be named with it. Composed about 1732,
of all Bach's secular compositions it comes nearest to a stage
operetta. The libretto is a tolerant skit upon the prevalent
coffee-drinking habit. The characters are Schlendrian, his
daughter Lieschen, a confirmed coffee-bibber, and a tenor
narrator. The dialogue is brisk. Unawed by other penalties
threatened by her father, a stern prohibitionist, Lieschen is
induced to surrender her coffee under menaces of perpetual
spinsterhood. She circumvents her father, however, wins
a husband, and retains her coffee, by forcing her bridegroom
to consent in the marriage contract,

> That she may do as she thinks fit,
> And coffee, if she likes, may drink it.

The use of his daughter's pet name suggests that the sketch
originally was a domestic comedy played in Bach's household,
the more so because the humorous *dénoûement* appears to
have been his own addition to Picander's text. Enlarged by
the addition of a ballet and other movements, the operetta
was produced by the British National Opera Company in
1925 under the title *Coffee and Cupid.*

Bach's semi-official connexion with the University invited
Academic him occasionally to provide music for academic
cantatas celebrations. Two works of that kind—*Der zufriedengestellte Aeolus* and *Vereinigte Zwietracht*—have been
mentioned among his 'Drama' compositions. Another is
the cantata *Die Freude reget sich*, performed about 1733 as
a birthday greeting from his students to Professor Johann
Florens Rivinus, with whom, as godfather of his youngest
son, the 'English Bach', Bach was on intimate terms. The
work is scored for a chamber orchestra, soprano, alto, and
tenor solos, and chorus. The text is conventional, and the
music adapted. Bach had used it at Cöthen in 1726 to
celebrate the birthday of Prince Leopold's second wife.
He employed its music again in the cantata *Schwingt
freudig euch empor*, and, as its text reveals, for an academic,

but unknown, occasion. Another adapted 'gratulation' score is that of *O angenehme Melodei*, whose arias he borrowed from *O holder Tag*, which honoured Count von Flemming, his Dresden patron, in whose house he routed the Frenchman Louis Marchand in 1717. The adaptation apparently was his last work on a secular score.

It was customary for the well-to-do to entertain their wedding guests with cantata music, the provision of *Wedding* which, at Leipzig, was Bach's prerogative. His *cantatas* 'Coffee Cantata' may at some time have been used for the purpose, and three others are extant. The earliest, *Weichet nur, betrübte Schatten*, was written at Cöthen, for what occasion is not known. It is for a soprano voice—probably his second wife's, Anna Magdalena—and a chamber orchestra. Similarly planned is the lately recovered *Vergnügte Pleissen-Stadt*, composed for the wedding of a Leipzig merchant and his Zittau bride on 5 February 1728. It is scored for two voices, a soprano and an alto, the former representing Zittau in the character of Neisse, her river, the latter speaking for Leipzig in the character of Pleisse, her chief stream. The third example, *O holder Tag*, has been mentioned already as the source of the music of *O angenehme Melodei*. It was composed about 1746: its libretto indicates that the bridegroom was a generous patron of music.

For the wedding ceremony of his daughter Lieschen Bach probably arranged the 'Three Wedding Chorals'. For the family celebration on the occasion of his own, some forty years earlier, he revised a score of greater interest and different character. It is a Quodlibet, unfortunately incomplete, for four voices and harpsichord accompaniment. A *Quod-* Quodlibet is a combination or *pot-pourri* of popular *libet* melodies, either arranged to sound simultaneously, or strung together in succession. Bach's wedding Quodlibet is of the latter kind. It includes some twenty tunes, sung consecutively without connecting interludes. The fugue which ended the work, unhappily, is lost, as also is the opening section. On the testimony of Forkel, the Bachs particularly delighted in this jovial and intricate exercise, and indulged in it with mirth at their family gatherings. Here is an authentic example! Its melodies, however, cannot be traced to a popular source, and the words are not traditional. The music is certainly by Bach himself.

At some undecided period Bach set three Italian texts to *Italian* music, two of which are extant—*Amore traditore* and *cantatas Non sa che sia dolore*. They are of genuine *cantata da camera* form, the first for a bass, the second for a soprano voice. The circumstances of their composition are not known. Similar doubt attaches to *Ich bin in mir vergnügt*, the last in this tale of Bach's secular compositions. It can be dated about 1730 and is scored for a chamber orchestra and soprano voice. Probably it was written for Anna Magdalena, for its sentiments truly express the happy contentment of Bach's domestic life.

Though they show how indefinite was the borderline between the two, Bach's secular cantatas, on the whole, are less interesting than those he wrote for the church, partly because his heart was with the latter rather than the former, also because even his indomitable spirit could not indefinitely suffer the conventional banalities he was invited to clothe with music. But the seriousness with which he treated them reveals the sturdy integrity of his character, and the music itself is, not seldom, the merriment of a very human soul.

NOTE

For an English translation of Bach's secular texts see the present writer's *Bach's Cantata Texts*. Their music is discussed by Spitta, *passim*; Schweitzer, vol. ii, chap. 30; Parry, chap. 9. For the Quodlibet see *Music and Letters*, vol. xiv, no. 1.

TABLE I

THE ORGAN MUSIC

No.	Subject	Period 1700–1708	Period 1708–1717 (Weimar) (a) Miscellaneous	Period 1723–1750 (Leipzig)
1	Allabreve	… … … …	D ma. (B.G. XXXVIII; N. II. 26; A. III. 435)	
1	Canzona	… … … …	D mi. (B.G. XXXVIII; N. II. 34; A. III. 441)	
5	Fantasias	B mi. (B.G. XXXVIII; N. XII. 71; A. V. 656) C ma. (B.G. XXXVIII; N. XII. 92; A. V. 661) G ma. (B.G. XXXVIII; N. XII. 75; A. V. 630) G ma. (B.G. XXXVIII; N. IX. 168; A. III. 453)	C mi. (B.G. XXXVIII; N. III. 57; A. III. 448)	
1	Passacaglia	… … … …	C mi. (B.G. XV; N. X. 214; A. III. 382)	
1	Pastorale	… … … …	F ma. (B.G. XXXVIII; N. XII. 102; A. V. 676)	
4	Preludes	C ma. (B.G. XXXVIII; N. XII. 91; A. V. 686) G ma. (B.G. XXXVIII; N. II. 30; A. V. 664) A mi. (B.G. XXXVIII; N. X. 238; A. V. 624) C ma. (B.G. XXXVI, No. 21; N. XII. 94; A. V. 1103)	… …	…
6	Sonatas (Trios)	… …	…	Eb ma., C mi., D mi., E mi., C ma., G ma. (B.G. XV; N. IV and V; A. IV)

A indicates the Augener Edition of Bach's Organ Works (which includes two fugues in C ma. (X. 1420) and G mi. (X. 1384) not included above. B.G. indicates the Bachgesellschaft Edition of Bach's Organ Works. In addition to the works named in the Table, B.G. XXXVIII in Appendix I gives an unfinished Fantasia in C ma., an unfinished Fugue in C mi., and an unfinished pedal exercise in G mi. Appendix II prints three Fugues of doubtful authenticity, in C ma. (A. X. 1420), D ma., and G mi. (N. II. 41; A. X. 1384). N indicates the Novello Edition of Bach's Organ Works (omitting, as not authenticated, the Fugues in II. 41; XII. 100; also the Prelude in C ma. (XII. 94), transferred from the Clavier music.

TABLE I

No.	Subject	Period 1700–1708	Period 1708–1717 (*Weimar*)	Period 1723–1750 (*Leipzig*)
3	Trios	...	*(a) Miscellaneous* D mi. (B.G. XXXVIII; N. II. 54; A. V. 688) C mi. (B.G. XXXVIII; N. XII. 108; A. IX. 1173) Aria in F ma. (B.G. XXXVIII; N. XII. 112; A. IX. 1178)	
4	Concertos (Vivaldi and others)	... ...	*(b) Arrangements* G ma., A mi., C ma., C ma. (B.G. XXXVIII; N. XI; A. V) *(c) Preludes (Fantasias, Toccatas) and Fugues*	
7	Fugues	C mi. (B.G. XXXVIII; N. XII; 95; A. III. 428) G ma. (B.G. XXXVIII; N. XII. 86; A. V. 669) D ma. (B.G. XXXVIII; N. XII. 83; A. IX. 1168)	C mi. (B.G. XXXVIII; N. X. 230; A. III. 412) G ma. (B.G. XXXVIII; N. XII. 55; A.V. 618) G mi. (B.G. XXXVIII; N. III. 84; A. III. 406) B mi. (B.G. XXXVIII; N. III. 60; A. III. 422)	
3	Fantasias and Fugues	A mi. (B.G. XXXVIII; N. XII. 60; A. V. 640)	C mi. (B.G. XXXVIII; N. III. 76; A. II. 215) G mi. (the 'Great') (B.G. XV; N. VIII. 127; A. II. 254) (?1720) D ma. (B.G. XV; N. VI. 10; A. I. 22)	
26	Preludes and Fugues	C ma. (B.G. XV; N. VII. 74; A. II. 157) C mi. (B.G. XXXVIII; N. II. 48; A. I. 124) A mi. (B.G. XXXVIII; N. X. 208; A. V. 612) E mi. (the 'Short') (B.G. XV; N. II. 44; A. I. 39)	F mi. (B.G. XV; N. VI. 21; A. I. 45) G mi. (B.G. XV; N. VIII. 120; A. I. 9) A ma. (B.G. XV; N. III. 64; A. II. 187) G ma. (the 'Great') (B.G. XV; N. VIII. 112; A. I. 56) A mi. (the 'Great') (B.G. XV; N. VII. 42; A. I. 83) C mi. (the 'Great') (B.G. XV; N. VII. 64; A. II. 168)	D mi. (B.G. XV; N. IX. 150; A. I. 100) orig. for violin B mi. (the 'Great') (B.G. XV; N. VII. 52; A. II. 198) C ma. (the 'Great') (B.G. XV; N. IX. 156; A. I. 69) E mi. (the 'Great') (B.G. XV; N. VIII. 98; A. II. 227) E♭ ma. (B.G. III; N. VI. 28; A. I. 133)

5 Toccatas and Fugues — E ma. (B.G. XV; N. VIII. 88 (in C); A. IX. 1185 (in C); A. II. 288)

C ma. (B.G. XV; N. III. 70; A. I. 1);
G ma. (B.G. XXXVIII; N. VII. 80; A. I. 112)
Eight Short Preludes and Fugues C ma., D mi., E mi., F ma., G ma., G mi., A mi., Bb ma. (B.G. XXXVIII; N. I; A. IV)
D mi (the Dorian) (B.G. XV; N. X. 196; A. III. 360)
F ma. (the 'Great') (B.G. XV; N. IX. 176; A. III. 331)
C ma. (the 'Great') (B.G. XV; N. IX. 137; A. II. 306)
D mi. (B.G. XV; N. VI. 2; A. II. 271)

(d) Choral Preludes

46 The Little Book for the Organ (Orgel-büchlein) — (B.G. XXV (2); N. XV; A. VIII. X)

6 The Schübler Chorals — (B.G. XXV (2); N. XVI; A. VII; VIII. X)

18 The Eighteen Preludes — (B.G. XXV (2); N. XVII; A. VI; VII. X)

21 The Catechism Preludes — (B.G. III; N. XVI; A. I; VI; VII; VIII)

24 The Kirnberger Preludes
28 Miscellaneous Preludes — These Preludes are of no particular period (B.G. XL; N. XVIII; XIX; A. VI; VII; VIII; IX; X)

(e) Choral Variations

4 — Christ, der du bist der helle Tag (B.G. XL; N. XIX. 36; A. IX. 1201)
O Gott, du frommer Gott (B.G. XL; N. XIX. 44; A. IX. 1210)
Sei gegrüsset, Jesu gütig (B.G. XL; N. XIX. 55; A. IX. 1222)

Vom Himmel hoch, da komm ich her (B.G. XL; N. XIX. 73; A. X. 1288)

TABLE II
THE CLAVIER AND CEMBALO MUSIC

No.	Subject	Period 1700–1708	Period 1708–1717 (*Weimar*)	Period 1717–1723 (*Cöthen*)	Period 1723–1750 (*Leipzig*)
			(a) Arrangements		
1	Adagio (3rd Sonata Solo Violin)	..	..	..	
16	Concertos (after Vivaldi and others)	..	G ma. (B.G. XLII; Bu. XI, XII)	..	G ma. (B.G. XLII; Bi. VII. 52)
2	Fugue (after J. A. Reinken)	..	Bb ma. (B.G. XLII; Bu. XX. 28)	..	
	(after J. C. Erselius)	..	Bb ma. (B.G. XLII; Bu. XX. 34)	..	
3	Sonata (after J. A. Reinken)	..	A mi.(B.G. XLII; Bi. IV. 50; Bu. XXV. 1)	..	
	" (after J. A. Reinken)	..	C. ma. (B.G. XLII; Bi. IV. 64; Bu. XXV. 18)	..	
	" (2nd Sonata Solo Violin)	..	..	..	D mi. (B.G. XLII; Bi. IV. 71; Bu. XXIV. 55)
1	Suite (3rd Partita Solo Violin) (*See also* Prelude and Fugue in E flat and Suites in E minor and C minor)	..	..	..	E ma. (B.G. XLII; Bu. XXIV. 23)
			(b) Concerto		
1	Concerto in the Italian style (*Clavierübung* II)	..	..	..	F ma.(B.G. III; Bi. I. 40; Bu. XIII. 1; Au. 8022)
			(c) Fantasias and Preludes		
6	Fantasia (and unfinished Fugue)	C mi.(B.G. XXXVI. No. 27; Bi. VII. 36; Bu. XXII. 2)	..	..	C mi. (B.G. XXXVI. No. 25; Bi. I. 107; Bu. XIV. 46; Au. 8022)
	"	..	G mi. (B.G. XXXVI; Bi. VII. 38; Bu. XXII. 11)	..	
	" (Prelude)	..	A mi. (B.G. XXXVI; Bi. VII. 40; Bu. XXII. 18)	..	
	" (on a Rondo)	C mi. (B.G. XXXVI. No. 26; Bu. XXII. 4)	..	..	
	Prelude (Fantasia)	C mi. (B.G. XXXVI. No. 22)	..	..	
			(d) Fantasias and Fugues		
3	Fantasia and Fugue	..	..	A mi. (B.G. III; Bi. I. 100; Bu. XXI. 1; Au. 8022)	A mi. (B.G. XXXVI; Bi. I. 94; Bu. XVIII. 34)
	" "	..	..	D mi. (B.G. XXXVI; Bi. I. 110; Bu. XIV; Au. 8022)	
	Chromatic Fantasia and Fugue	..	..	..	

Au. indicates the Augener Edition. B.G. indicates the Bachgesellschaft Edition. B.G. XXXVI includes (No. 12) a Prelude and Fugue in E flat actually by Joh. Christoph Bach, of Eisenach, and (App. II. No. 2) the fragment of a Suite in A major actually by Telemann. Both are omitted from the Table. B.G. XLII contains an Appendix of fifteen compositions of doubtful authenticity, of which No. 11 (Suite in B flat major) is alone admitted to the Table. B.G. XLIV (1) prints four Inventions wrongly attributed to Bach (see p. 28 *supra*). Bi. indicates the Steingräber Edition, edited by Hans Bischoff. Bu. indicates the Breitkopf Edition, edited by Ferrucio Busoni.

TABLE II

THE CLAVIER AND CEMBALO MUSIC

No.	Subject	Period 1700–1708	Period 1708–1717 (*Weimar*)	Period 1717–1723 (*Cöthen*)	Period 1723–1750 (*Leipzig*)
				(h) Prelude and Fughettas	
4	Prelude and Fughetta	D mi. (B.G. XXXVI; Bi. VII. 118; Bu. XX. 1; Au. 802o[3], p. 34)			
	″ ″	E mi. (B.G. XXXVI; Bi. VII. 120; Bu. XX. 5; Au. 802o[3], p. 38)			
	″ ″	F ma. (B.G. XXXVI; Bu. XX. 12)			
	″ ″	G ma. (B.G. XXXVI; Bu. XX. 16)			
				(i) Preludes and Fugues	
3	Prelude and Fugue	A mi. (B.G. XXXVI; Bi. VII. 128; Bu. XIX. 21; Au. 802o[3], p. 45)		A mi. (B.G. XXXVI; Bi. VII. 131; Bu. XIX. 6)	E♭ ma. (B.G. XLV (1); Bi. VII. 144; Bu. XIV. 61)
	″ ″				E mi. (B.G. XLV (1); Bi. VII. 54; Bu. XXIII. 1)
	″ ″ (cembalo or lute)				C mi. (B.G. XLV (1); Bu. XXIII. 11)
			(k) Sonatas		
2	Sonata	D ma. (B.G. XXXVI; Bu. XXIV. 45)	A mi. (B.G. XXXVI; Bi. II (1) 52; Bu. XXIV. 2)		
	″ (one movement)	A mi. (B.G. XLV (1))	E♭ ma. (B.G. XXXVI; Bi. II (1) 58; Bu. XXIV. 11)		
			F ma. (B.G. XXXVI; Bi. VII. 62; Bu. XXIII. 40)		
			(l) Suites		
19	Suite				
	″				
	″ (Ouverture)				
	Suite (Lute)				
	″ (Lute)				
	″ (probably authentic)			B♭ ma. (B.G. XLII; Bu. XXIII. 30)	
	Six French Suites			D mi. (B.G. XLV (1); Bi. II (1); Bu. VI; Au. 8021)	
	″ ″			C mi. (B.G. XLV (1); Bi. II (1); Bu. VI; Au. 8021)	
	″ ″			B mi. (B.G. XLV (1); Bi. II (1); Bu. VI; Au. 8021)	
	″ ″			E♭ ma. (B.G. XLV (1); Bi. II (1); Bu. VI; Au. 8021)	
	″ ″			G ma. (B.G. XLV (1); Bi. II (1); Bu. VI; Au. 8021)	
	″ ″			E ma. (B.G. XLV (1); Bi. II (1); Bu. VI; Au. 8021)	
	Six English Suites			A ma. (B.G. XLV (2); Bu. VII; Au. 8017[a])	
	″ ″			A mi. (B.G. XLV (1); Bi. II (2); Bu. VII; Au. 8017[a])	
	″ ″			G mi. (B.G. XLV (1); Bi. II (2); Bu. VII; Au. 8017[a])	
	″ ″			F ma. (B.G. XLV (1); Bi. II (2); Bu. VII; Au. 8017[b])	
	″ ″			E mi. (B.G. XLV (1); Bi. II (2); Bu. VIII; Au. 8017[b])	
	″ ″			D mi. (B.G. XLV (1); Bi. II (2); Bu. VIII; Au. 8017[b])	

	Reference
Unfinished Suite (3 movements)	F mi. (B.G. XXXVI; Bi. VII. 68; Bu. XXIII. 48;
7 Toccata	D ma. (B.G. XXXVI; Bi. I. 82; Bu. XVII. 31)
,,	D mi. (B.G. XXXVI; Bi. I. 70; Bu. XVII. 49; Au. 7983)
,,	E mi. (B.G. XXXVI; Bi. IV. 93; Bu. XVIII. 1; Au. 7983)
,,	G mi. (B.G. XXXVI; Bi. IV. 100; Bu. XVIII. 10)
,,	G ma. (B.G. XXXVI; Bi. IV. 85; Bu. XVIII. 21)
,,	F♯ mi. (B.G. III; Bi. I. 52; Bu. XVII. 2; Au. 7983)
,,	C mi. (B.G. III; Bi. I. 60; Bu. XVII. 16; Au. 7983)

(m) Toccatas — G ma. (B.G. III; Bi. IV. 14; Bu. XV)

	Reference
2 Aria variata	A mi. (B.G. XXXVI; Bi. VII. 45; Bu. XVI. 28)

(n) Variations

	Reference
Aria with 30 variations (Goldberg) (*Clavierübung IV*)	G mi. (B.G. XLV (1))

(o) Miscellaneous

	Reference
Allemande (W. F. Bach's *Little Clavier Book*)	G mi. (B.G. XLV (1))
Allemande (W. F. Bach's *Little Clavier Book*)	
Capriccio (for Joh. Jakob Bach)	B♭ ma. (B.G. XXXVI; Bi. VII. 24; Bu. XIV. 31)
,, (for Joh. Christoph Bach)	E ma. (B.G. XXXVI; Bi. VII. 30; Bu. XXV. 52)
Four Duets (*Clavierübung* III)	(B.G. III; Bi. IV. 5; Bu. III)
Marches (A. M. Bach's *Note-book* 1725)	(B.G. XLIII (2))
Minuets (A. M. Bach's *Note-book* 1725)	(B.G. XLIII (2))
Minuets (one in duplicate) (W. F. Bach's *Little Clavier Book*)	(B.G. XXXVI and XLV (1); Bi. VII. 22; Bu. XXV. 65)
Minuet-Trio (W. F. Bach's *Little Clavier Book*)	(B.G. XLV (1))
Musette (A. M. Bach's *Note-book* 1725)	(B.G. XLIII (2))
Polonaises (A. M. Bach's *Note-book* 1725)	(B.G. XLIII (2))
Cembalo Solo (A. M. Bach's *Note-book* 1725)	(B.G. XLIII (2))
Duet for two Claviers	F ma. (B.G. XLIII (1))?

Au. indicates the Augener Edition. B.G. indicates the Bachgesellschaft Edition. B.G. XXXVI includes (No. 12) a Prelude and Fugue in E flat actually by Joh. Christoph Bach, of Eisenach, and (App. II. No. 2) the fragment of a Suite in A major actually by Telemann. Both are omitted from the Table. B.G. XLII contains an Appendix of fifteen compositions of doubtful authenticity, of which No. 11 (Suite in B flat major) is alone admitted to the Table. B.G. XLV (1; prints four Inventions wrongly attributed to Bach (see p. 28 *supra*). Bi. indicates the Steingräber Edition, edited by Hans Bischoff. Bu. indicates the Breitkopf Edition, edited by Ferruccio Busoni.

TABLE III

THE CHAMBER MUSIC

No.	Subject	Period 1717–1723 (Cöthen)	Period 1723–1750 (Leipzig)
		(a) Instrumental Solos	
6	Sonata, Violin	G mi. (B.G. XXVII (1); P. 228ᵃ)	
	Partita ,, 1	B mi. ,, ,,	
	Sonata ,, 2	A mi. ,, ,,	
	Partita	D mi. ,, ,,	
	Sonata ,, 3	C ma. ,, ,,	
	Partita	E ma. ,, ,,	
6	Suite (Sonata) Violoncello	G ma. (B.G. XXVII (1); P. 238)	
	,, ,,	D mi. ,, ,,	
	,, ,,	C ma. ,, ,,	
	,, ,,	E♭ ma. ,, ,,	
	,, ,,	C mi. ,, ,,	
	,, ,, ('a cinq acordes')	D ma. ,, ,,	
		(b) Instrumental Solos with Continuo accompaniment	
3	Sonata, Flute	C ma. (B.G. XLIII (1); P. 235)	
	,, ,,	E mi. ,, ,,	
	,, ,,	E ma. ,, ,,	
		(c) Sonatas for two Instruments and Continuo	
2	Sonata, Violin	E mi. (B.G. XLIII (1); P. 236)	
	,, ,, 1	G ma. (New B.G. XXX. No. 1)	
1	Fugue, Violin	G mi. (B.G. XLIII (1); P. 236)	
1	2 Violins-Continuo	C ma. (B.G. IX; P. 237)	
2	Flute-Violin-Continuo 2	G ma. (B.G. IX; P. 237)	

1 See the Cembalo and Clavier Table: Sonata in D minor.
2 See the Cembalo and Clavier Table: Adagio G ma.
3 See the Cembalo and Clavier Table: Suite E ma. (Arrangements).

1 On the same bass as the Sonata for Flute, Violin, and Continuo in the same key (*infra*).
2 On the same bass as the Violin Sonata in the same key (*supra*).

B.G. indicates the Bachgesellschaft Edition.   P. indicates the Peters Edition of Bach's Chamber Music.

2	Flute-Violin-Continuo	G ma. (B.G. IX; P. 239)	..	..
1	2 Flutes-Cembalo [3]	..	..	C mi. (B.G. XXXI (2); P. 237)
1	Canon Flute-Violin-Continuo [4]	..	..	C mi. (B.G. XXXI (2); P. 237)

(d) Sonatas for Cembalo and one Instrument

3	Cembalo-Flute	B mi.	(B.G. IX; P. 234)
	"	A ma.	(" " "
	"	E♭ ma.	(" " "
6	Cembalo-Violin	B mi.	(B.G. IX; P. 232)
	"	A ma.	" " "
	"	E ma.	" " "
	"	C mi.	" " 233)
	"	F mi.	" " "
	" [5]	G ma.	" " "

[3] The probably earlier form of the Cembalo-Gamba Trio in the same key.
[4] The fragment of a Trio in F major for Violin, Oboe, Continuo, is in B.G. XXIX, p. 250.
[5] A seventh Sonata for Cembalo-Violin, in G mi., is in B.G. IX, p. 274 (P. 3068). If genuine, it is an early work.

1	Cembalo-Violin (Suite)	A ma.	(B.G. IX; P. 236)
3	Cembalo-Gamba [1]	G ma.	(B.G. IX; P. 239)
	"	D mi.	(" " "
	"	G mi.	(" " "

(e) Concertos

7	Cembalo (Strings, Cont.)	..	..	..	..	D mi.	(B.G. XVII; P. 254)[2]
	"	"				E ma.	" " 253)
	"	" [3]				D ma.	" " 251)
	"	"				A ma.	" " 252)

[1] In a probably earlier form as a Sonata for 2 Flutes and Cembalo (supra).
[2] Perhaps originally composed for a viola d'amore. Cf. B.-J. 1931, p. 143.
[3] Also as the Violin Concerto in E ma. (infra).

7	Cembalo (Strings, Cont.)[1]	..	..	..	..	G mi.	(B.G. XVII; P. 249)
	"	"				F mi.	" " 250)
3	2 Cembali (Strings, Cont.)[2]	..	..	..	..	F ma.	" " 248)
	"	" [3]				C mi.	(B.G. XXI (2); P. 257)
	"	"				C ma.	" " 256)
	"	"				C mi.	" " 231)[a]

[1] Also as Violin Concerto in A mi. (infra).   [2] Also as the fourth Brandenburg Concerto in G ma. (infra).
[3] Also as the Concerto for 2 Violins in D mi. (infra).

TABLE III

THE CHAMBER MUSIC

No.	SUBJECT	PERIOD 1717–1723 (*Cöthen*)	PERIOD 1723–1750 (*Leipzig*)
2	3 Cembali (Strings, Cont.)	.. .. ..	D mi. (B.G. XXXI (3); P. 258)
			C ma. " 259)
			A mi. (B.G. XLIII (1); P. 260)
1	4 Cembali (Strings, Cont.)[4]	.. ..	
1	Cembali, Flute, Violin (Strings, Cont.)	A mi. (B.G. XVII; P. 255)	
3	Violin (Strings, Cont.)[5][6]	A mi. (B.G. XXI (1); P. 229[a])	
		E ma. (B.G. XXI (1); P. 230[a])	
	" (3 Trombe, Timp., 2 Ob., Strings, Cont.)[7]		
1	2 Violins (Strings, Cont.)[8]	D mi. (B.G. XXI (1); P. 231) ..	D ma. (B.G. XXI (1))

[4] An arrangement of a Concerto for 4 Violins by Vivaldi in B mi.
[5] Also as G mi. Cembalo Concerto (*supra*). [6] Also as D ma. Cembalo Concerto (*supra*).
[7] 'Sinfonia,' incomplete. From a lost Cantata. [8] Also as the Concerto for 2 Cembali in C mi. (*supra*).

6	Brandenburg Concertos:		
(1)	Violino piccolo (Horns, Oboes, Bassoon, Strings)	F ma.[1] (B.G. XIX; P. 261)	
(2)	Violin, Trumpet, Flute, Oboe, Violin (Strings)	F ma. " 262)	
(3)	Strings	G ma. " 263)	
(4)	Violin (Flutes, Strings)	G ma.[2] " 264)	
(5)	Cembalo, Flute, Violin (Strings)	D ma. " 265)	
(6)	Strings	B♭ ma. " 266)	

(f) Ouvertures (Suites)

4	Ouverture	C ma. (B.G. XXXI (1); P. 267)	D ma. (B.G. XXXI (1); P. 269)
	"	B mi. " 268)?	D ma. " 2o68)
	" 3		

[1] Also, shortened, as a Sinfonia in F ma. (B.G. XXXI (1)).
[2] Also as the Cembalo Concerto in F ma. (*supra*).
[3] B.G. XLV (1), p. 190, prints an unauthenticated Ouverture in G mi.

B.G. indicates the Bachgesellschaft Edition.
P. indicates the Peters Edition of Bach's Chamber Music.